THE
SIX
HABITS

By
Laura DiBenedetto

ISBN 978-1-7347043-1-0 Hardback

ISBN 978-1-7347043-2-7 Downloadable audio file

ISBN 978-1-7347043-0-3 Ebook

ISBN 978-1-7347043-3-4 Paperback

Published by Laura DiBenedetto, Inc. | 1254 S. Kihei Rd. #2210, Kihei, HI 96753, USA

DEDICATION

This book is dedicated to my parents. I wouldn't be who I am if it wasn't for you. Everything you went through, hardships you endured, and all the lessons you gave me (intentional or otherwise) were not in vain. I am a happy, healthy, complete person because of everything we've shared. I love you, and I admire who you are as individuals and as a package deal. If you've ever doubted yourself as parents, here it is in black-and-white: you are my perfectly imperfect parents, and you've done an extraordinary job. Thank you for showing me what perseverance, commitment, and integrity look like. Thank you for teaching me to appreciate the little things in life, which is the origin of everything that came bursting out of me in these pages. Most of all, thank you for always choosing me and being truly unconditional with your love. Your presence in my life has always been (and continues to be) a gift that I never take for granted.

This book is further dedicated to my husband and my closest friends, people who love me not in spite of my deep, dark, and ugly things, but because of them. Thank you for allowing me to be myself, loving me as-is, and making my life even better by being in it. Thank you so much for choosing me to be part of your life. I want to thank you for putting your faith in me, giving me ninety days, and working to help me prove the success of all the principles.

Finally, this book is dedicated to you, the reader. I never knew what I was meant to do in life, but I always knew it had something to do with making people happy. I hope this book does that, and the lessons contained within help you to smile for the rest of your life. Thank you for giving me this chance to make your life better.

TABLE OF CONTENTS

LET'S DIVE IN

2 | The Six Habits

Being unhappy is optional. I've had a wealth of experience that gave me all of the tools I ever needed to be an unstoppable force of nature… and yet, one day while working on something that would make me really happy, I was filled with crippling self-doubt and *I stopped*. Again! After all that work, after all those years of therapy, coaching, personal development books, seminars, great ideas, chats with friends, journaling, meditating, affirming, and you-name-it, I was still unhappy—and let my limiting self-beliefs stop me dead in my tracks for the umpteenth time.

What. The. HELL!?

In response to yet another halted journey and out of sheer frustration, I set out on a course to find out why and solve the problem permanently. This book holds the solution. I wrote this book so I could share it with you. If you're like me, you've probably done some great things in your life, have a good idea of what to do to *not* be unhappy, and yet…you still end up feeling pretty unhappy anyway. This book is for the intelligent person (both you and me!) who has already tried the book, the exercises, the courses, etc., and is already aware of some of the things it takes to get there. For whatever reason, you've struggled to develop any permanency with feeling fantastic, capable, and more than anything, sticking with it.

This is the book about replacing the six specific harmful habits most of us have with the opposing, life-giving ones that the most happy and successful people already have deeply ingrained. Even more than that, this is a book about changing your relationship with yourself so you can change your relationship with your whole world. The relationship we have with ourselves determines our journey in life. If you generally think poorly of yourself, treat yourself poorly, and are an aimless, ungrateful, distracted ball of toxic energy—you're not going anywhere in life. Conversely, if you think well of yourself, treat yourself with love, have purpose and direction, are grateful, focused and positive, baby, you're going places—*fast*.

The challenge we all face when it comes to our habits is that we tend to know one thing but do another. For example, we all know we should floss after every meal. Yet, most of us don't. It's not because we don't know any better. We simply didn't acquire the habit of doing it. Sure, it may happen occasionally (as needed), but that's not a habit. A habit is something you do regularly and automatically without conscious thought required to make you do it. The fact is, we don't stick with the things we know are good for us because we haven't developed the muscle to do it.

The trouble with not sticking with things we know work, is that it robs us of the courage to live the life that would most make us happy. It seems trite to say that happiness is the key to everything, but it really is. Buddha once said, "There is no path to happiness: happiness is the path." I couldn't agree more. Happiness begets courage, courage begets confidence, confidence begets happiness. I'm not that person that buys into "bumper sticker psychology," and there are many personal development books out there that just aren't real or grounded, despite the core nuggets of wisdom. I'm not religious and I can't get behind books that are written in a super fluffy way with lots of God talk and filled with prayer. Those books have a place in the world, without question, but just not a place in my hands. I've always believed that God helps those who help themselves. So, this is me, helping *myself* and giving you the tools while asking you to help *yourself*. I'm giving you some straight talk to help you get out of your own way once and for all.

As you read this book, you may find some parts of this obvious and others will give you a sorely needed epiphany. If we were friends in real life, you'd know me as the friend with the reputation for speaking the truth on a regular basis (that's one of *my* deeply ingrained habits). I'm the one who will tell you there's broccoli in your teeth, the one who will tell you that the dress *does* make you look fat, and I will tell you when things *aren't* going to be okay, confirming that you really screwed up. At the same time, I'm the one who will hand you a toothpick and a mirror, I'll help you get a new dress to slay and strut your stuff like a runway model, help you fix your epic mistakes, and stand by you the whole time. Yeah. I'm *that* friend.

Surface conversations and shallow relationships are boring to me. They always have been. You don't get to talk about the real stuff going on, you don't share the things you're scared of, your innermost thoughts, and most definitely not your shortcomings. With this book, you and I are entering into a deep relationship, a relationship with some of my "deep, dark, and uglies." This is an intimate relationship with your real truth, and your own culpability. The great part about a book is that it's a safe, one-way relationship. I'm going to share some frank truth about me, my own insecurities, the things that scare me, and some of the painful experiences that have helped shape who I am. Through my revelations, you're going to see just another imperfect human being that desperately wants to live an amazing life, that wants to be loved, and that's sick of stopping herself—and finally has. You never have to reveal the truth about your insecurities and fears to me, or anyone else if you don't want to.

As a friend of mine said more than once, "When Laura DiBenedetto loves you, she loves you all the way." I can't help but nod in agreement. This book is me loving you all the way.

WHAT TO EXPECT

When we do the internal work to become our biggest, brightest selves, life changes for the better all around. Most of us have something that's *broken* in our relationship with ourselves. Whatever is broken is that which stands between us and the life we most desire. If we ever hope to have what we desire in any tangible way beyond just wishing for it, we need to focus inward. It is then our own responsibility to find what's broken within and repair it. I intend to help you do just that. I'm going to guide you through The Six Habits, as well as the logic and approach to each one. I will also share tangible stories that bring each habit to life.

You'll find and see that the pathway to healing our relationship with ourselves is simple, but not easy. I've loaded this book with challenges and exercises to make it as easy as it could ever be. They're sprinkled liberally throughout the book. Have your notebook ready. With these challenges, you need to show up for yourself. It's on you to do the work so you can *apply* this knowledge and begin your journey of mastery starting now. What good is the cure for a disease if it's never used?

As I was writing this book, I built lots of *free* companion tools to help you *apply* everything I'm teaching you so you can master The Six Habits. Everything I challenge you to do can be done in a notebook, but the tools I've built for you are more organized and in-depth, offering you a helping hand to make sure you succeed. Don't be shy—go online and help yourself to all my tools and bonus material at thesixhabits. com/resources. If you don't feel like doing it now, don't worry. I'll remind you periodically throughout the book whenever I'm encouraging you to do something.

Let's get started by specifically naming what's possible for *you* as a *result* of your mastery of each of these habits.

BY MASTERING THE FIRST HABIT, YOU WILL

- » Upgrade your internal monologue to be encouraging and nurturing as your default.

- » Take bold action, enjoying the giddy pursuit of life-long dreams, and empowering self-belief.

- » Feel worthy, confident, capable, and courageous regularly.

- » Advocate for yourself, no longer tolerating mistreatment from others.

- » Notice self-destructive habits and work to eliminate them.

BY MASTERING THE SECOND HABIT, YOU WILL

- » Stop comparing yourself to others, finally

believing that you are enough.

» Feel deep, authentic contentment with and appreciation for who you are.

» Stop needing to prove yourself, engaging in destructive behaviors, letting others take advantage, or apologizing for your wants and needs.

» Give yourself permission to be, do, and express who you truly are.

» Experience improved relationships in love, family, friendships, and work.

BY MASTERING THE THIRD HABIT, YOU WILL

» Experience life through the enhanced lens of appreciation, objectivity, curiosity, and learning.

» Heal old wounds, reframe painful memories, and find the good in difficult situations.

» Bounce back from painful moments faster and with greater resilience.

» Grow as a person and finally tap into your potential for greatness.

» Experience deeper and more intimate romantic relationships, more meaningful friendships and family relationships, in addition to more dimensional and powerful professional relationships.

BY MASTERING THE FOURTH HABIT, YOU WILL

» Relax with ease more often and have loads more fun.

» Easily redirect your focus from the past or the future.

» Experience your life consciously, coming off unconscious autopilot.

» No longer suffer the loss of precious time captivated by vices and distractions.

» Intentionally design and live fully into moments that inspire you.

BY MASTERING THE FIFTH HABIT, YOU WILL

» Become conscious and protective of your energy.

» Prioritize things that contribute to your wellbeing and actively focus on them.

» Safeguard yourself against toxic people, toxic situations, and toxic vices.

» Accurately prioritize what's important in your life, deriving deeper joy from every day.

» Stop missing out on the things that matter to you.

BY MASTERING THE SIXTH HABIT, YOU WILL

» Get clear about what you want in life and why.

» Set realistic, measurable, attainable goals for yourself—and achieve them.

» Gain the power and courage to take massive action toward what you want.

» Stay on course with your action plan when life threatens to derail you.

» Have the courage to do the things that scare you.

THE OVERALL EFFECT

The impact of mastering The Six Habits can be dramatic and broad. These habits cover the full breadth of your life, not just one aspect of it. Whatever you're trying to manifest in your life, your habits are what will bring it all together for you. Maybe you want to start a business, lose weight, fix a broken relationship, get married, be a more involved parent, or just be happier. You can create whatever you want, but it requires *mastery* of the *right* habits. Your *current* habits are what got you to where you are now. When you want more or better, you have to *be* better first.

Your habits define your relationship with yourself, and your relationship with yourself defines your life.

THE BACKSTORY

I came into the world in the middle of a snowstorm at the tail end of 1980 to parents that *really* wanted me. My mother suffered two miscarriages before I came onto the scene, and even through her seventh month of pregnancy with me, she didn't dare dream she'd get to be a mom. Not to spoil the ending or anything, but I did indeed show up.

I was far from being an easy baby, and though she'll never admit it, I'm pretty sure I made her regret her decision to be a mom on hundreds of occasions. My lucky parents got to deal with a hyperactive baby that wouldn't hold still and had the will to do what she wanted with the ferocity of a rabid dog. As I grew older, I always had double the energy of a normal kid. I was louder, messier, more stubborn, and significantly more frustrating than I think my parents bargained for. Having ADHD (Attention Deficit Hyperactivity Disorder) will do that to a kid. I was also hyper-emotional, lost my cool when I couldn't have what I wanted, and refused to do what I was told. But wait—there's more. I was an extreme slob, I was rude, and I couldn't pay attention to anything that wasn't genuinely fascinating—like school, chores, or anything involving responsibility.

Coupled with being poor (Dad was and still is disabled) and being an only child, I was somewhat of a "different" kid and didn't really have friends. The only friends I had mistreated me. As I'm writing this, I'm struggling to think of one kid that was my genuine friend, and I can't think of a single one. Having no friends wasn't the problem. When I tried to socialize with neighborhood kids, I was bullied and ridiculed. They never wanted to play with me, and when they did, it was to use me for something I had that they didn't have (like my backyard, which was perfect for sledding). I was always the outcast, and when I tried *not* to be, it backfired.

When I tried to socialize with kids at school, I was tormented endlessly about my appearance, physically assaulted, made fun of for everything imaginable, and was again the outcast. I got used to it, but this kind of sweeping rejection did a number on my budding psyche. Like all kids, in my tender formative years, I didn't have the capacity to sort it all out or understand it. It just hurt. It left me feeling like, "all the kids hate me; so, I hate myself too."

Growing into a teenager wasn't much fun either. While the physical assaults came to an end, I got treated the same lousy way by older kids whose insults had become more articulate and creative. I was a late bloomer into adolescence and was still flat-chested when other girls were sporting D-cups. I dressed awkwardly, I didn't know how to do my hair, and I was covered in freckles that literally nobody else in the entire school had. Although I was clean, I didn't smell amazing because we had a fireplace with a crack in the chimney that we couldn't afford to fix. That crack produced creosote, a foul-smelling black tar made up of smoke and water, and the smell clung to my clothes.

I didn't know how to talk to anyone except adults. I liked boys who most certainly didn't like me back, and the mere thought of me liking them made them pretend to vomit out of humiliation. I was a social leper. My grades were amazing in precisely half of my classes, and I was borderline failing the other half—the half less interesting. I most certainly didn't like who I was at that point in my life because there was nothing *to* like. I had one boyfriend in my junior year of high school, only to have him dump me because I wouldn't have sex with him before I was ready. After enduring even more years of rejection, I contemplated suicide constantly, believing that I was worthless, but since I hated the sight of blood (thank goodness I'm a wuss!), I never actually tried.

Take all of this, put it all together, and upon graduation, you've got an angry, rude kid with zero desire to live, resentment for everyone and everything, and abundant self-loathing. I didn't believe I had any value. I didn't believe I could do anything or was worthy of anything. I had no people skills, didn't know how to build relationships, didn't know how to have a friend or be a friend, and didn't know how the world worked.

I went to college and had a slightly different experience than primary school, but it didn't vary much. The principal difference in the college environment was that it was much easier to disappear into obscurity, and I was all too happy to let it swallow me whole.

I got several part-time jobs, and my life began to change, but not necessarily for the better. It just became different. Although it *appeared* better, it wasn't. I started working hard at my jobs and saw the value of hard work firsthand. I wasn't well-liked at work either, but I got a paycheck at the end of the week and had something to show for all the work and the frustration.

My second job was at an upscale billiard hall as a cocktail waitress, where I was exposed to a lot of older people, specifically men. Now, this is where my psyche took an unexpected turn. With years and years of self-loathing, believing I was worthless, unattractive, and an outcast, being thrown into an environment with lots of inebriated men gave me an entirely different (although skewed) worldview. I brought them drinks, they tipped me well, they complimented me, flirted with me, and *desired* me. For the first time in my life, I *didn't* feel rejected. Instead, I felt valued, important, and wanted. Unfortunately, it was for all the wrong reasons and I couldn't see that at the time.

I interpreted that my worth was defined by what men thought of me and their use for me. I got more dates than I knew what to do with. I had a wine glass I kept on the coffee table in my dorm and it was jammed with phone numbers. I went on date after date, but they all ended the same way. I was eighteen and still a virgin. This discovery was either met with running away: "I don't want to be the one," or haphazard disregard for my feelings: "You should totally have your first time be a one-night stand."

What I didn't understand at the time was that these dates were *not* originated from a place of mutual respect. There were no goals of finding a girlfriend or a long-term companion. Instead, these were dates that wanted me for only one thing. I was feeding into this manipulation without realizing it. I thought their interests and affections were the real deal, but they were a façade. I couldn't tell the difference or discern that there even was one to look for. Thus, I faced more rejection. My self-esteem couldn't plummet because I didn't have any to begin with. In my head, I internalized this all to mean that I still wasn't good enough. I continued to hate myself and deeply crave the acceptance and love I'd been denied my whole life.

Across all those years, I want to be clear that my parents' love never wavered. They always unconditionally loved me, accepted me, and did everything humanly possible to make my world a good one. That's what good parents do, and they were the very definition of good parents. The trouble is, much to the chagrin of good parents everywhere, the world is comprised of more than just our loving parents and kind-hearted people. It was a painful place for me. My immature mind twisted the actions of selfish people into false ideas of truth and my place in the world—ideas my parents couldn't help me overcome.

When I came home from school with tears in my eyes and rips in my clothes from being shoved down on the playground, my parents told me repeatedly how worthy, interesting, kind, and sweet I was. They cuddled me and made their arms the only safe place in the world. Their embrace and physical affection spoke louder than anything they ever verbalized because it touched a part of me words couldn't reach. I never forgot how they made me feel. Unfortunately, their incredible love and efforts weren't enough to undo everyone else's impact on me, which wasn't their fault. The world wasn't kind to me, they couldn't stop it, and my development into adulthood was less than ideal.

My first serious relationship came about when I was nineteen. He was thirty-eight. I know, I know. At the time, that large, waving red flag wasn't visible to me. I met this guy at work, and he was like all the other men I'd gone on dates with, except he genuinely enjoyed my company. He wanted to be around me, we did fun things, and even though he insisted, "I don't want to be the one," and "I don't want to be remembered," he eventually changed his mind—so did I. He was my first, and he was as angry and bitter in life as I was. I innocently thought I was the one person that would be safe from his rage. Ah, to be so young and naïve again.

I ended up verbally abused when it was just the two of us, and when his friends or customers were around. He humiliated me often and liked to remind me that I was young, stupid, and his property. I was physically abused when no one was looking because I dared to speak my mind and have my own ideas about how things should be. He terrorized me. I was sexually abused and made to do things I didn't want to do, things I didn't know anything about.

I didn't know any better. After all, he was my first. I had no frame of reference for sex beyond him. I let all of it happen, thinking this was the only way I would ever receive love, and this was the best I could hope for. I put up with it until one day he got physical again, nearly breaking a bone, and I couldn't take it anymore. My self-worth was at its lowest point, and I was positively indifferent toward myself (hating yourself requires caring). I was just plain scared for whatever painful encounter would come next. I was so beaten down that I almost stayed, but it was the fear that helped me leave.

After enduring a lifetime of abuse and rejection by what felt like everyone, and then a significant other, I'd had enough. I left. I sat in the silent aftermath: bitter, broken, angry, rejected, and confused. I stayed at my parents' house for a few months and basically stared at the wall for days at a time. My mind began to repair itself, and in the safety of my parents' home, hiding from the world I hated so much, I started to sort out what I could. At twenty, I didn't have the wisdom I do now, of course. However, my intuition told me over and over that what I'd been through was deeply wrong and I could have a different life than the one I'd been living. I felt miserable. At that moment, I *knew* that being unhappy and *feeling miserable was optional*, and every day since has been a battle to choose anything but the unhappiness. I was angry as hell that other people robbed me of my happiness, and worse—*I let them.*

Shortly thereafter, while not having any luck finding a decent job, I got a small business off the ground. Once that was going, I found an apartment that I was *mostly* sure I could afford, I got the world's best cat (seriously, he was amazing), and I started going to therapy on my own. I wanted to feel good and continue to feel good, so I started doing the work to fix my mixed-up headspace. I was tired of hating myself and didn't see the point in it anymore. Once you innately understand that being unhappy is an entirely controllable choice, it's tough to go back to the ignorance of thinking it's out of your hands and you have no say in the matter.

For a few years after I left the abusive relationship, I dated in a healthier way, but those relationships didn't work out. At twenty-three, however, I met someone I liked right away. I felt a surge of love, affection, safety, acceptance and everything I ever wanted, so I did the unthinkable: I married him eight weeks after I met him. You read that right. Eight. *Eight measly weeks.*

Was I crazy? Yes! I look back now and think: WHAT? I'd like to say I married him so quickly because I was confident he was right for me, knew him well, and had learned so much about him that it was clearly a good decision. But that's not the case. I married him because of the love, affection, safety, and acceptance that I felt *of course*, but in a big way, I was afraid someone so great would leave me. I didn't want to bother "looking under the hood." I thought this was the best chance at happiness I'd ever have, and I didn't want to risk *not* taking my chance on being happy. He was the first (non-parent) person that ever truly loved me, was kind to me, showed me affection for real, and made me feel safe. It might surprise you to learn (heck, me too), that my impulsive first marriage lasted ten years, seven of which were pretty good. At the end, we both left the marriage as much healthier, happier, more complete people than when we entered it.

I don't regret it.

Over the years, I struggled to maintain my weight, hated how I looked, struggled to stick with any habit longer than a few weeks, and I started more projects than I can even count—I finished maybe 10% of them. I was a late bloomer to a dozen things that many of my peers had known for years. I got married in five minutes, got a divorce, was impulsive and rash in my many of my decisions, went bankrupt and lost my home, lost thousands of dollars to poor business decisions, and have essentially fallen flat on my face hundreds if not thousands of times. I've condemned myself for being an epic failure nearly every time and hated myself the whole way.

Know what's great about failure? You get numb to it after a while, and you don't mind failing anymore because you don't care so much eventually. You just pop back up every time. Even better than that, you learn new things at a rapid pace and constantly improve. That in mind, in time, I stopped condemning myself, and I stopped making my failures more than what they were.

WHY I CAN HELP YOU

Throughout my adulthood, I worked on my relationship with myself. I always knew that better was possible, and I never gave up on the idea. Through my first marriage and after, I always saw progress, no matter how small, and got better all the time. It was slow going with ups and downs, but it *was* going. I didn't realize that the things I was doing right were The Six Habits, and because I didn't realize that, I wasn't consistent, hence the slow pace. Once I figured it all out, I started quantum leaping. You will too.

Despite the negative things I shared with you, I've had a great deal of tremendous success in almost every area of my life because I pushed hard for what I wanted. I did what worked because I knew *it was all a choice* and I desperately wanted to create my own happiness and success. I refused to give up on myself. That little small business I started at nineteen blossomed into what we see today: a full-service marketing company with a powerful team and dozens of clients that love us. I retired from active involvement in late 2018 after nineteen years of working hard, and now, someone else continues to manage the day-to-day for me.

In 2019, I sold my large home in Massachusetts and fulfilled my lifelong dream of moving to a tropical island. I now enjoy warm breezes, relaxing walks on the beach, and dazzling sunsets whenever I want on the beautiful island of Maui. I wake up without an alarm clock. I travel internationally frequently and used to take roughly eight weeks off a year. Now I take time off whenever I choose. I have a satisfying amount of money in the bank and across my investment portfolio. I've finished some amazing projects, I'm in a wonderful marriage that makes me feel happy and fulfilled, and more important than any other thing I've listed: I finally mastered the habits required to genuinely like who I am and know I am worthy of love. Now I will fight to the death for my right to be happy and love myself. It was through The Six Habits that I finally healed my relationship with myself once and for all and gained the courage to check some pretty big boxes on my dreams list.

Despite my limiting self-beliefs, despite the years of rejection, and despite everything in my DNA that wanted me to always make the wrong choice, I've frequently made the right choices. I've kicked some serious butt, and it was always because of the *same good habits* time and time again.

So, that's a great tidy ending, right? I'm all better? I'm

perfect now?

Nope. Sorry, I'm still human, and I'm still lugging around that baggage from the past, as much as I try not to. It's lighter than it was, but it's still there, playing a role in my psyche, attempting to shape my decision-making processes, my habits, and my actions. I choose to continue to work on myself every day, and it gets easier all the time. I make conscious choices where my habits aren't quite fully developed so I can be my highest and best self.

I continued to struggle for years in *sticking with the right habits* so I could make more of the right choices on a more consistent basis. That was the entire motivation behind this book. I wanted to get out of my own way to identify and then stick to the good things that have consistently proven to give me a better life. I was tired of having fits and starts of success, and the occasional hot streak in the middle of a long slog of uphill battles. I knew there had to be a better way, and I was right.

In the summer of 2018, right before I retired, I was burned out, tired, and sick to death of not feeling the consistent high of joy and success I knew was possible. I had tasted it so many times, had accomplished many things, but I still wasn't happy and was facing the fact that my "What's next" plan for after retirement was shaping up to be something I didn't want. Despite massive investments and so much dreaming and doing, I had to start over. I had dreamed of opening an upscale European bakery in the Boston area and had to admit that the more I got into it, worked on it, and invested into it, the unhappier I was. I had picked the wrong dream, or perhaps the wrong time and place. Either way, I was miserable. You'd think that being on the brink of retirement, I'd be elated. I wish. Sitting still has never been easy (ADHD, remember?), and I wanted a "What's next" plan to get excited about. Abandoning it when I could see it wasn't going to make me happy was the right thing to do, but it crushed me anyway.

I'm grateful I was crushed. This book, all of my resources online, and The Six Habits 90 Day Habit Mastery program all exist because of it. You see, abandoning the business I thought I really wanted to create was the final, fatal blow to the lies I was telling myself about how happy I was. I'd bought the house, I had the great husband, I went on the trips and did all the things I felt I was supposed to do, but I wasn't truly happy. I was beaten, tired, and sick of being alive. My vacations were more about escape than joy. My home was a trophy that was a pain in the butt to clean. The money was great, and I spent a lot of it on stupid stuff I never touched twice. It was painful to admit, but true.

For about fifteen years, I had been an ever-increasingly huge fan of personal development. I went to classes, workshops, week-long events led by big-name leaders, and retreats. I read dozens of books. I meditated. I journaled. I did challenges. As amazing as it all was, none of it stuck and I couldn't figure out what was working and what wasn't. *That* was the problem I wanted to solve. No, *needed* to solve. Like I said earlier, the obstacle we all face when it comes to our habits is that we tend to know one thing but do another. The fact is, again, we just don't stick with the things we know are good for us because we haven't developed the muscle to do it.

I knew this and started digging into my own habits, the habits of others, the science, the research, and everything I could get my hot little hands on so I could make *myself* feel better consistently. This book exists because I found the *real* secret to actual lasting happiness, the secret that can bring any possibility to life. What I found worked so well in making me feel better, that my whole life changed! I started sharing what I found and changing lives around me. I found my purpose in life, and most importantly, I healed and reshaped my entire relationship with *me*. The secret? You're holding it. It's The Six Habits.

The Six Habits is not about changing yourself. I'm still me, and you'll still be you. The Six Habits is about changing your habits and the things you automatically do and think in the small moments day-to-day. When you develop new automatic and positive habits in the six key areas I'm going to share with you, you change the scope of possibilities for your entire life. I did. The people who have read my book before you and applied my teachings have done it. You, my amazing friend, will too.

I want to be clear about one critical thing before we go any further. *I am nobody special, and I do not have something that you don't have.* Read that again! I massively and radically changed my life, my attitude, my happiness, and all that life could give me, and *so can you.* I did it as an average human with the same head trash we all have, along with the disadvantages, baggage, and trauma you read about earlier.

My being no one special is an important point that I need you to retain as you read this book and do the challenges.

Being special doesn't define outcome here—effort does. Reading this book and not *applying* what you learn will keep you where you are.

Too often we see our heroes in the spotlight, and we silently conclude they're better than us somehow, or they have something inside of them that we *don't* or *can't* have. That is a *lie* we tell ourselves because we can't put our finger on what it is that gets them the grand life we admire. I'm telling you what it is, and I'm putting your finger on it. They have their *habits*, and by the end of this book, you'll be on your way to cultivating the very same habits your heroes put to work every day to put them where they are in life—and I'm going to show you how to do it.

NOT TOMORROW. TODAY!

What I know for sure is this: misery knows no prejudice. You can be poor and kicked around like me, or you can be the rich popular kid that has it all. It doesn't matter because we all have our issues, and if you're feeling miserable, then there's a good chance you don't want to be. Misery is the great equalizer. It doesn't matter what your background is, what you look like, how much money is in the bank, how talented you are, or whether you're married or alone. Think about Robin Williams, Kate Spade, or Anthony Bourdain. These incredible people seemed to have it all. If you feel miserable, and I'd argue that many of us do some or most of the time, your position in life isn't worth a hill of beans when it comes to finding the way out. You can't *buy* your way out, you can't *drink* your way out, you can't *exercise* your way out, and you can't even *think* your way out. We all have but one path: *do the work and <u>earn</u> the way out.*

Whatever you're going through, whatever your cross to bear happens to be, you have the opportunity to be happy. We've got one brief life on this amazing planet of ours, and you could get trampled by an angry water buffalo that just escaped from the zoo tomorrow. Or you know, hit by a bus. Do you really want to waste whatever time you have left choosing to be unhappy? I don't.

I'm sorry to be so blunt about it, but you're going to die someday, and you don't know when. I realize that's an unpleasant thought. The mere thought of it *really* messes with me, and I can barely reckon with the idea, but seriously, it's freeing when you realize how fleeting life really is, and how you're messing up your one precious life by staying in your own way. Think on this in earnest for a moment. You could *for real* die tomorrow. It could just as likely be next year from surprise cancer, or it could be seven years from now because you choked on your dinner. It could be eighteen years from now due to heart disease, or you could die nice and old in your sleep. You don't know when and how, but you most certainly will die. This is an unavoidable truth.

Imagine for a moment that someone you know died. Let's call him Mike. Mike was always wallowing in self-doubt, self-pity, and never got out of his own way. He never took big risks, he never had the cake, he never tried to open that business he dreamed of, he rarely took vacations, he never liked himself, and always thought everyone else was more deserving. He "got by" and seemed to only be focused on surviving the week until Friday came, and the misery would always set in again by Sunday night. Mike was nice to everyone but himself. He was a genuinely good person and it was easy to see. His attitude toward his dreams was always, "someday." Then one day, Mike suddenly died, and someday never came. Upon Mike's death, you'd most likely be thinking how tragic *his life* was *because he never really lived it*. The death wasn't the real tragedy —his life was. Do you want that to be *YOU*?

Of course you don't. I'm here to help. Together, we're going to change your life. I promise. You will not be the one wallowing in self-doubt and self-pity. Baby, you *will* get out of your own way. No more "getting by." Not for you. You are going to learn to be nice to yourself and eat the cake. Your life is about to become cause for celebration and excitement. You deserve nothing less. You weren't put on this planet to apologize your life away, make excuses, or shrink back from everything you want. Nope. It's time for more.

You've been given one precious life, and you have the freedom to change your life whenever you want to by changing your *mind*. You can't change your past, you can't control the outside world, you can't control who wins the election, you can't control other people, you can't control the steady stream of negativity in the news, or all the horror that happens around us every day. But you *can* change your relationships with *yourself*, your *actions*, and your *reactions*. With this book, you *will*.

LIVING IN PAIN

Believe it or not, we opt *in* to our suffering. Worse, unhappy people don't accomplish a lot. We unconsciously choose to be unhappy when we know better is possible. We compare ourselves to others, we talk ourselves out of our dreams, we feel incapable, we tell ourselves that we don't look good and aren't enough. All of these things are heinous lies. They're a cluster of unnecessary and destructive cycles that obstruct our path to living amazing lives of inspiration and joy. The tinkerers and inventors of the world have long tried to invent the perpetual motion machine, not realizing we already have one in our heads and it's working quite well, unfortunately.

Instead of all that negativity, we truly can have, do, and *be* so much better. When we jump into the *possibility cycle*, we create happiness as well as possibility for our dreams. Let me explain the cycle. First, you can jump into it at any point. If you're feeling happy, it begets courage. If you're feeling courageous, you'll take action. If you're taking action, you'll feel satisfied with yourself. If you're feeling satisfied, that quite naturally leads to confidence. When you're feeling confident, you feel happy. While you *can* jump in anywhere, the most accessible point of entry for all of us is happiness. This is what we're working on right now in these pages.

Following this diagram, you can see what's truly possible

for you. Now imagine this as a repeating cycle. On your entry, you start at happiness, then onto courage, then action, then satisfaction, then confidence, and then with every new repeat of the cycle, you find a *higher level* of happiness. Yes, while you're back at the concept of happiness, you're experiencing it from a place of accomplishment that leads to new possibilities and new ways of understanding what happiness looks like in your own life. Once you've experienced a more profound sense of happiness, you can't *unknow* it. You will always know it and will always know what it feels like. You'll start to reframe your baseline expectations of what happiness looks like and you will have newer, more powerful "bare minimum" requirements for how you want to live.

If you love this graphic and want to keep it front-and-center, head to thesixhabits.com/resources for the mini-poster.

Mastery of this life-giving cycle begins with understanding that our critical responsibility throughout all of The Six Habits is twofold: self-awareness, and self-regulation. It's our job (and no one else's) to recognize what we're doing that's harmful to ourselves, it's our job to give ourselves the new information to change it, and finally, it's our job to *powerfully* redirect ourselves to the good things that will change everything.

In this book, we talk about The Six Habits that create life-long happiness. Six simple things. So, what could be so complicated? Why don't we know this already? Why don't we do it already if we do know it?

The fact is, we've spent our whole lives becoming

incredibly good at choosing the wrong things, reinforcing negative thought-processes and habits, and believing our own lies. I've done it, you've done it, we've all done it. It's never going to happen overnight for anyone, but we all have the capacity to learn to choose the right things, to reinforce positive thought-processes and habits, and to learn not to believe our own lies.

Through The Six Habits, you will change your life. You will succeed based on the fact that they *are* so simple. Once you know them, you'll become more self-aware and your ability to lovingly self-regulate will develop into loving, lasting habits that will permanently change your life from what it was into what you've always wanted it to be.

WHEN WE'RE MEAN TO OURSELVES

We're all mean to ourselves at one point or another: you, me, the neighbor, the person you think is really stuck up, and your heroes. All of us. When we aren't kind to ourselves, we hold ourselves back from reaching our highest potential. We'll say and think mean things to ourselves about our performance, our capabilities, our achievements, our appearance, our health, our relationships, our value, our dreams, and more.

When we continually reinforce our negative thoughts, it leads to fear and hesitation (self-doubt), which can manifest itself in some ugly ways: our relationships can suffer, we can be more sensitive and not bring our best selves to conquering challenges with our loved ones, we can give up on ourselves, and sometimes not even try. Sound familiar? When that happens, we feel bad about ourselves and the *negativity cycle* begins all over again. We stay firmly planted in the exact place we don't want to be, or worse, lower.

Entering the negativity cycle typically begins with self-loathing and shame. This self-loathing and shame work so well that you progress automatically to the next step of negative self-talk, which is the beginning of the all-too-familiar routine of saying terrible things about yourself in your head or out loud. Naturally, this hurts, and it's quite effective. Sadly, because it works so well, you then move automatically to the next step, feeling fear and hesitation.

You have quite successfully beaten yourself down lower and no longer have courage or conviction. From there, you take yet another crushing step into inaction—the death of your dreams, and the death of possibility. Just when you think you can't go any further, you take one more step, this one familiar: self-loathing and shame all over again. Without intervention, this continues endlessly.

When we aren't kind to others, it is *we* who suffer the most. Our hearts carry the burden of judgment, anger, and resentment, and we can't let things go. We feel guilt, shame, and stress for nothing. It creates so much negativity in our hearts and influences how we treat others, and ourselves.

WHEN WE WISH OURSELVES
(AND OTHERS) WERE DIFFERENT

Struggling to accept ourselves is part of the human condition. It's quite easy to fall into the cycle and never come out. Unfortunately, it's normal in our society to wish we were someone or something we aren't. We often want to be more than we are and find our current selves *"as is"* to be insufficient. We frequently wish to be smaller, thinner, stronger, smarter, richer, more powerful, more beautiful, more handsome, more influential, more popular, etc. Endless product companies rely on this negative self-judgment to sell the next great magic goo or system, taking our money and leaving us feeling still broken and worthless inside. Tragic evidence of this is all over mainstream media, advertisements, and social media. We all struggle with this to varying degrees at one point or another in our lives.

When we find ourselves in this cycle, we're failing to (or refusing to) accept ourselves. We're holding an idealized version of ourselves in our mind (wishing and hoping we were *something* or *someone* else) and can't *forgive* ourselves or *love* ourselves for being anything other than the idealized version we imagine. This happens because we've bought into the idea that in order to be *enough* or *worthy*, we must be different than who we truly are—that other people have it right, and we don't. Further, through this buy-in, we've come to believe we are broken and need fixing. Some of us unconsciously take this one step further. We accept the next thought that if we are broken and need fixing, there is no point in trying, and therefore, we are worthless, disposable, and can never be enough.

While seeking to improve, working on ourselves, or growing as a human is healthy and deeply rewarding, it *must* be done from a place of love and appreciation for where and who we are now. When the improvements, work, or growth happens from a place of love and joy, it's healthy and nurturing. It can unlock many doors.

However, when the improvements, work, or growth happens from a place of *refusal* to truly love or accept ourselves, these activities are sly disguises for what they really are: refusal to be who we are and a desperate bid to be anyone else we feel is more *worthy* of love. When this happens, we're often faced with the harsh reality of our unmet expectations of ourselves as compared to the ideal version we envision, which organically leads to disappointment in ourselves, potentially on a grand scale. The natural result is dissatisfaction, and from there, we end up wishing and hoping all over again. So, it continues.

Accepting others is hard to do when we can barely accept ourselves, and it exists in the same crushing cycle. If you don't believe how destructive it is when we fail to accept others, look at the divorce rates in the United States and the staggering amount of bad news. We wish and hope that others are a certain way. When we discover they are *not* what we wish and hope, through our perception of their "failure" (valid or otherwise), our unmet expectations of them lead to disappointment, which creates dissatisfaction in the relationship, and the wishing and hoping begins all over again.

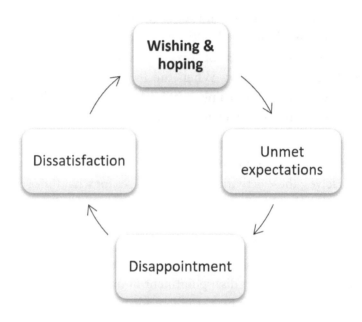

WHEN WE TAKE PEOPLE & THINGS FOR GRANTED

When we take the good things in our lives for granted, stop appreciating the blessings we have, and fail to find the good in bad situations we should be grateful for, we fail to maintain a healthy and positive perspective. We see the world through the "glass half empty" perspective, and always easily find what's wrong in life instead of what's right with it.

This perspective hinders our abilities to do simple things like getting out of bed with a "can do" attitude, and all the way up to starting a company or asking the one you love to marry you.

The concept of gratitude seems simple: be grateful for your blessings. However, the role gratitude plays in our lives is much grander. When we take things for granted, expectation sets in and we forget that our blessings are a privilege, not a right. We even stop seeing them all together. When we live in the state of expectation (and then life happens as it does), this leads to inevitable disappointment when we don't get what we expected, and usually, that's accompanied by genuine shock and anger. These negative feelings organically breed resentment and bitterness, which by default, leads to unhappiness, which in turn leads to more lack of appreciation.

When we aren't grateful for the vast array of blessings we have in our lives, our worldview is bleak and depressing. When we only see the bad in a negative situation and refuse to acknowledge the lessons waiting for us within, we can't learn or grow. When we fail to appreciate the many gifts that *we* have that so many others *wish* for (like a job, a family, or health), we descend into an unconscious mindset of privilege that breaks our connection with humanity.

Lack of gratitude for *all* of life, inclusive of its ups and downs, makes it hard to get out of bed every day with any sense of gusto, purpose, or interest. It's just another day and you're waiting to die, *not* excited to live. With this lack of gratitude, it's next to impossible to feel good about ourselves, it's hard to appreciate anything or anyone, and we have a black cloud over our heads that we can't even see. It's too easy to get caught up in taking ourselves, our lives, our blessings, and others for granted, and the downward spiral from there is debilitating.

WHEN WE'RE DISTRACTED

We're all guilty of being distracted. From texting when we're out to dinner with our loved ones, to watching television and not paying attention when we're at home with the kids, to checking Facebook constantly when we're at work—we're pretty checked out. Worse yet, we're focused on the victories and failures of yesterday, and the hopes and fears of tomorrow. When we're checked out, we're missing out on what's happening right here and now, and we can't enjoy it, learn from it, or feel good.

We're living in a time when cell phones don't seem to exist for *our* convenience anymore. Instead, they seem to exist for the convenience of those who wish to reach us, including those who make money off of our attention. Our bosses or customers expect connectivity and access, so do our families and friends. We're expected to always be "on," always reply quickly to any question, email, or text, and to stay "up to date." Even as I write this, I feel the pressure of "feeding the beast" of Instagram to keep up with the algorithm so my content is shown to my own audience. The information stream is literally endless, and we cannot keep up with what's happening. There is intense pressure on most of us just from the *Internet* alone to stay connected and "on."

On top of all that, when we factor in the notions of past and future, our ability to be present doesn't stand a chance. If all that is combined with habitual unkindness to ourselves, lack of gratitude, and a generous helping of toxicity all around us, we can't enjoy our lives.

By choosing to live in the past, future, or something other than what our attention would be better invested into, we're allowing ourselves to be distracted. It means we're not present, and we're missing out on the here and now. Often, this becomes a destructive habit we indulge in every day. We know how much it hurts us, and we can't or won't stop the distractions because the allure of the past, future, phones, TV, or anything else, is too tempting.

One day, when we realize what we're missing out on, we'll become disappointed with ourselves (whether we realize it or not), and it leads to more "self-medicating" behaviors of distraction (like smoking, drugs, alcohol, social media addiction, or worse). Like the other hurtful concepts here, this too is a cycle.

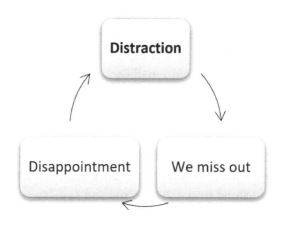

WHEN WE GET STUCK IN NEGATIVITY

Humans are funny creatures, aren't we? We say we want to be happy, but judging by our actions, it looks like we want anything but. We feed on negative energy like the hungry caterpillar feeds on leaves and it does an incredible amount of invisible damage to our worldview.

Think about your experiences with social media, when you interact with draining people, when you see horrible stories in the news, or when you read an article that shows you how disgraceful our world can be. There's no denying it's incredibly negative and fills you with all kinds of bad feelings. When was the last time you watched a news story on the six o'clock news about someone getting murdered and jumped up from your couch to cheerfully pursue your goals? Oh right, that didn't happen—because it doesn't.

You're not alone. All this negativity organically leads to unconscious, swirling negative feelings in all of us that the world is bad, people are bad, situations are bad, and it can never be good. It gets worse. From there we tend to seek confirmation of our feelings either by gossiping about others, consuming more hurtful media through social channels, the TV news channels, mass media, and whatever else it takes to confirm our bleak worldview. Yes, it gets even worse. We even go so far as to justify our behaviors as "need," thereby defending the negative input, powerfully ensuring the stream of negativity never stops flowing. We firmly stay in the cycle, essentially swirling the drain.

With all of this negativity, it's next to impossible to feel like anything new, good, extraordinary or out-of-your-comfort zone is *possible* in your life, never mind practical or attainable. This cycle of negative energy consumption is one that kills possibility before possibility ever has a chance to grow roots within us. This cycle breeds feelings of apathy, disinterest, depression, disconnection, and hopelessness.

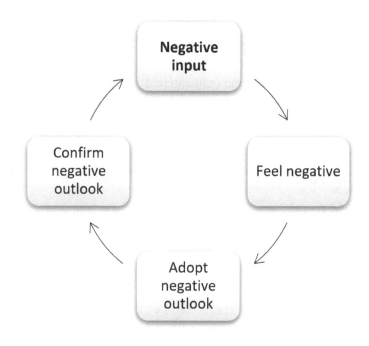

WHEN WE'RE A PASSENGER IN OUR OWN LIVES

Drifting through a life we didn't exactly intend to be living is far too common. Maybe it's a marriage that's uninspiring, unromantic, fraternal, and never going anywhere, but we stick with it anyway out of a perceived sense of obligation. Perhaps it's a job that leaves us feeling largely underwhelmed, underpaid, and seriously underappreciated, but we stay because it's so much easier than upsetting the apple cart. Maybe it's the dream we never try to pursue because we don't know how to do it, we don't believe we'll be successful, and we defeatedly convince ourselves that our dreams are better lived out by other, more capable people. In any case, all of this leads to us "going with the flow" and drifting through life without a firm grip on our own life's steering wheel.

When we're this rudderless, we're not in control of our lives. Our circumstances and the natural cause and effect of going with "whichever way the wind is blowing" is what controls us, and our life's course. Again, *we* are not in control.

This invariably leads to abandonment of dreams for who we could become, what we want to do, and the lives we *could* be leading—the very lives we spend hours wishing for. When we let go of these dreams, the natural consequence is that we're filled with regret and self-loathing. Our inner selves are so disappointed by our actions, and the lack thereof, that the disappointment is palpable. Then we begin to believe these new terrible stories about what we can and can't do—and they're all a lie. The wheels fall off when we start to interpret these lies as *new* truths about who we are and our supposed limitations. Now we're back at the beginning, just going with the flow all over again, drifting along and helpless.

When you go with the flow instead of actively creating and designing your own life, you're just like a sad little kid who got told they *couldn't* go to the playground. You're the kid sitting in the back of the family car steered by someone else, feeling defeated, dejected, victimized, and miserable. *This* is how dreams die.

LIVING IN JOY

Change doesn't occur over a lifetime. Change occurs in an instant. It begins with a decision. *The decision is the change.* The decision is the day and the exact moment when you realize you've finally had enough of all the cycles of negativity and want to get off the hamster wheel once and for all. That day is a tremendously important day in your life. I might argue that it's more important than your wedding day or the day you start your dream job because it's the day you *finally* decide to love yourself. This is the day you *finally* decide you're worthy of your dreams and can't take *not* having them come true one more day. This is the day you *finally* understand that better is possible, *you can* actually have it, and will.

I pray this day is *today* because this amazing day is a pivotal one, and it's so exciting. When you work on yourself, you build yourself, and you purposefully create yourself, you are better all around. You're better in your marriage, your job, your parenting, your friendships, your ambitions, your dreams, your presence in the world—all because you decided to be. The list of benefits is truly endless, and *you* are the beneficiary of it all.

The moment the pain of staying still is greater than the pain of change, is the moment *you* change. This moment, the one where you are reading these words, is the one you can choose to learn the tools to create life-long happiness and empowerment for yourself (and by default, others too). You're about to learn what's been messing you up and how to fix it. You're about to learn how to build new habits you'll stick with because they feel great, and you *want* to stick with them. You're going to learn how to redirect yourself with love and clarity when the inner critic shows up again. Most importantly, you'll learn how to go the distance and push past your former limiting self-beliefs.

This is a big day, and this is a pivotal moment. Are you ready?

THE SIX HABITS

1. Kindness

Kindness is the habit governing self-relationships and the starting point for self-regulation. It is the habit of choosing to build rather than destroy, to be mindful in thought, speech, and action throughout everyday life.

KINDNESS TO YOURSELF

The subject of kindness is twofold: kindness to yourself, and kindness to others. Kindness to yourself, much like acceptance, is a challenge for most. Kindness to others is pretty easy (sociopaths notwithstanding). Let's look at being kind to ourselves first. It's harder to do but helps you to be kinder to others, so let's start there.

Being kind to myself is not something I have been routinely good at up until I discovered The Six Habits and put them into practice. Not only did I not accept myself for who, what, and where I was in life, I was extra mean to myself about it. I treated myself badly through words, thoughts, and deeds. I would constantly beat myself up for never being as successful as I should be, never being as pretty as I should be, never being as nice as I should be, or [fill in the blank] as I should be. The problem with these thoughts lies with

47

the word, "should." When you tell yourself that you should be anything or anyone other than exactly who and what you are, you are judging yourself and you set yourself up for failure. The only "should" you need to pay attention to? You *should* be exactly who you are and love yourself for it. Most importantly, you should *treat yourself accordingly.*

Kindness is behavior. Kindness is action. Kindness is *not* acceptance, but the two habits are connected and can be confused. Kindness is how you *treat* yourself; acceptance is how you *feel* about yourself. Acceptance is covered in the next chapter.

People struggle to deeply believe they are worthy in general, but particularly when it comes to kindness. Believing that you are worthy to the core of your being can be difficult to learn how to do, but not impossible. Constantly beating yourself up means you don't accept yourself and you're doing the opposite of kindness—which is being unkind to yourself. Acceptance, which we'll talk more about, is equally important.

To be kind to yourself is to be gentle with yourself. Often, we treat ourselves much worse than we would ever dream of treating someone else. We say terrible things to ourselves when we look in the mirror—Things like: "You're so fat," "That looks disgusting on you," "You look ugly," and so many other horrible things we would never dare say to another person. How can we be so horrible to ourselves? Why do we deserve less love from ourselves than the love we give to our friends, family, coworkers, bosses, clients, and everyone else? You wouldn't even say those horrible things to a complete stranger. I would argue that many people wouldn't even say those things to an enemy.

We say other horrible things to ourselves when we think about our performance: "You're so stupid, I can't believe you did that." When we fail, we might say, "Of course you failed. That's all you do." When thinking of going after that new client you want, your self-talk might sound like, "You'll never be able to make that sale, don't bother trying." Our brains are programmed with thoughts like, "I'm just a fool, what was I thinking when I ever thought for a moment that I deserved to have this?" When going after something we passionately want in life, we sabotage ourselves, thinking we don't deserve the things we have or the things we want.

We also say terrible things to ourselves when it comes to relationships. *We make our relationships worse because we refuse to be kind to ourselves.* Here's a great example: "He doesn't love me, he's just saying it to be nice," or "I don't *really* look good in this dress, he just doesn't want to hurt my feelings and tell me how bad I really look," or "That woman will never go out with me, so I don't want to even ask." Our unkind actions toward ourselves show up in our behavior and perception surrounding the people we love, and want to love. We end up bringing a huge bag of issues, assumptions, and toxic traits into our relationships—where they have no business being.

Are you seeing yet how absolutely horrible we are to ourselves? Do you see what it robs from us? Do you see how much flogging and abuse we tolerate from ourselves? We would never accept such hideous treatment from anyone else on the planet. Not our parents, not the ones we love, not our spouses, not our bosses, not our friends, not even strangers. No one! If we shouldn't tolerate this behavior from anyone else, and many of us wouldn't, why is it acceptable to tolerate this kind of abuse from ourselves?

When we fail to be kind to ourselves, there is no safe, pleasant, or neutral ground. You're either kind to yourself, or you're not. If you're not, you're a bully. You're no different than the angry big kid on the playground in school that likes to hurl insults and push the other kids down. Except you're the bully *and* the victim.

It's not just wrong, it's debilitating. How can you ever expect to go after the things you want in life if you constantly have this mean little bully inside your head giving you a constant stream of negative spirit-breaking lies about how ugly you are, how unlovable you are, how lazy you are, how much of a loser you are, how much you don't deserve it, etc.? We don't go after the things we want in life because we don't treat ourselves with kindness and give ourselves the loving encouragement we *need* to go get them. We don't become the people we want to become in life because we don't have the loving, nurturing acceptance and kindness in our heads that affords us the right to accept who we are.

When we succeed in being kind to ourselves, we are the *nurturing parent*. We are the voice of love, reason, encouragement, and reassurance. With this nurturing parent inside of us, the bully doesn't stand a chance and is always shooed away because the *action* of love is stronger.

I am your classic Type A overachiever. I certainly didn't arrive in life this way, but here I am. You'll soon see more about what I went through to become who I am. It wasn't pretty. What I failed to do for so many years was to be kind to myself. I always used my ambition and my drive as an excuse to beat myself up constantly. Without realizing it, all that negativity was the fuel in my gas tank.

Let me be the first one to tell you that it's tragic that I used negative reinforcement for so many years to get me where I wanted to go. It was painful, and *I achieved because of my self-loathing, not because of my self-love.* While I've gotten where I wanted to go, I didn't enjoy the journey, it took longer than it should have, and it was all uphill. Frankly, I found it hard to enjoy the results, and I also struggled to feel any source of pride or value when I surveyed my accomplishments. It is a process I have worked very hard to undo, to great success. The decision to be kind to myself happened in an instant, and thus began the change. Everything else fell like dominoes. I *now* love who I am, accept who I am, and have reframed my thinking, which is something you're going to learn how to do very soon! I am my *own* nurturing parent, speaking to myself with love and encouragement, saying uplifting and reassuring things to myself, and always standing up for my own success and joy. I deserve kindness and love. I don't need to apologize for deserving love from myself, any more than you need to apologize for deserving love from yourself. You are on your way to being your own nurturing parent.

Kindness is a practice. You must practice kindness for yourself with every moment, every word, and every thought. We expect this behavior of nurturing parents, and you need to expect this behavior of yourself.

At the end of 2017, I grew incredibly sick of being unkind to myself. I had just turned thirty-seven, and I decided I was going to do something that scared me. I was going to go on an international trip by myself, sit on the beach alone, and be with my thoughts. This might not be too crazy for some, but for me, the idea of solo travel to a country where I didn't speak the language sounded daunting. Nevertheless, I was willing to step outside of my comfort zone and go. I went to Cancun, Mexico, sampled extraordinary amounts of tacos without apology, and sat in solitude as I appreciated the turquoise water, the soft white beaches, every speck of nature I could find, and thoroughly explored the contents of my head.

I asked myself what I wanted most out of life, how I wanted to feel, what I definitely *didn't* want out of life, and what I most certainly did *not* want to feel anymore. I challenge you to do the same. I came back from my trip with two powerful and clear realizations. First, that I absolutely, and in all ways, needed to be kind to myself. It was no longer acceptable to be anything but. I would normally map out "SMART" goals for myself, but this was the first time I didn't. I simply said: "I wish to be kinder to myself," and made a sincere, heart-felt promise to myself that I would.

This promise was unlike most others I'd made in my life. This was a promise I knew to the marrow of my bones that I would not break. Many times, when I made myself a promise to hop on the next fad diet or any other thing, I had a little voice in the back of my head reminding me it was just a matter of time before I would fail —and I inevitably did.

I failed the fad diets and failed with the other promises to myself because my *reason* for making the promise in the first place wasn't compelling enough. *This* promise was different. *This reason* was different. I had finally decided I loved myself and would no longer bully myself after years of mistreatment and being fed lies about my value in the world. This promise stuck.

My first successes with kindness came right away. As I sat on the beach in Mexico in my two-piece bathing suit, with my belly fat squishing over the bottom of my bikini, I looked down and chose to laugh. I laughed with appreciation for a body that I built with joy. I ate food that I liked, and it made me happy. Why should I beat myself up for that choice? I shouldn't. I chose to go on a trip to a foreign country without my husband. Some people thought I was insane and disrespectful to my husband. I chose to politely and lovingly disagree, which was also kind to myself. That trip was a gift to and from myself—a gift my heart desperately needed. My trip brought me clarity, as solitude always does, and my husband not only supports me, but encourages me. Our marriage is one that encourages each other to live our best, most authentic lives. I will not apologize to myself or anyone else for choosing to live my best life and gain clarity. *None of us should*.

My second realization involved what I wanted to pursue next, and I knew the only way I would ever have *any* next career was by practicing kindness to myself and encouraging myself to get there. As we'll dive into shortly, my success in my first career was born out of necessity. I felt I had no other choice but to succeed. I had a choice with my next career, and I had the luxury of failure. Therefore, I knew instinctively I needed more grit and determination to do things because I deeply want to, not because I had to.

My first step was to observe. I needed to observe my triggers. I needed to learn where, why, when, and how I was unkind to myself. By listening to myself and hearing the bad things I said to myself, I would *then* be able to undo it. I listened carefully to everything I said. I was on high alert with self-awareness. I listened intently to the negative narrative in my head. I heard the evil words that came out of my mouth when I spoke to myself. I listened to the debilitating head trash around my job performance on the things that I thought I could and couldn't do. I also observed the discouraging things I was telling myself around career number two.

Through this observation I learned a very powerful thing: I was being a malicious bully to myself. As soon as I spotted this, I started to think of how I wanted to feel instead. I could see everything I was losing because I was being a bully, and what I stood to gain if I could get my head right and start being kinder to myself. The benefits of being kind to myself were clear: I would do more, be happier, take bigger risks, and push myself from a place of self-love, and belief. I wanted that for myself so badly.

The need for kindness in my own life is tremendous, and I will argue it's just as pressing in your life too. You need to be relentless to create the things you want in life, and I lost my ability to be relentless when I failed to be kind to myself. I had to start from zero and learn to be kind to myself, forgive myself, and most importantly, love myself. If not, I could kiss my dreams goodbye. When you create something out of need, you push because you don't really have much choice in the matter. When you create something out of love, you have to push from a different place. You *do* have a choice. You don't *need* it, so your pushing must come from a place of *desire*, which is wholly dependent upon self-kindness and self-belief. Without kindness, you just can't do it.

In total transparency, I am on the journey right next to you, and I have by no means fully "arrived" as a perfect deity of kindness sitting on my own personal mountaintop of glory. Sorry, nope! The bullying voices are still there. However, with every kindness, with every nurturing word, thought, and action, they get quieter and *eventually* go away. I have unlearned the old habit of being the bully to myself—it's no longer my default. The few stray bullying words, thoughts, and actions that still pop up are in the areas I haven't fully addressed yet because well, they're just less common in my life, and life is pretty broad. It's hard to squash a lifetime of mean thoughts instantly, but every time one of these nasty bullying thoughts comes up, I squash it and I triumph with love. How? I'm a ninja at redirecting my thoughts.

I became a kinder, more loving person to myself through redirection. The journey to effectively redirect has three important parts: catching the bad (the destruction), reminding myself of what I wanted and how to treat myself instead (the instruction), and reframing my thoughts or words (through construction). Through the process outlined under "Redirection," I promise you will learn to be kinder to yourself by daily practice. Kindness to oneself will lead to greater feelings of self-acceptance, personal joy, and feelings of capability and courage.

Since I began my journey of kindness to myself, I have experienced tremendous growth as a person. I'm happier down to the core of my being, and it shows up automatically. Here's what I got out of learning to be kinder to myself:

> » I finally like who I am as a person, with no motivation to be anything other than who I organically am. While the magazine covers might like to airbrush me, I don't want to. My "flaws" aren't flaws. They make me interesting and human. I love that.

> » I accept my failures, forgive myself for my mistakes, and I no longer beat myself up for them. I use failures as an exciting opportunity to learn and ask insightful questions. I look forward to sorting through the ashes of a failure to see what surprises are waiting for me so I can grow, get even better, and level up.

> » I've given up on trying to look perfect, I've accepted that no one does, and I've decided to stop hating my face and my body. Instead, I love it all, just the way it is. I don't weigh myself, I don't deny myself the ice cream, and incidentally, my attitude toward indulgence has changed from "I can't have it" to "I can have it whenever I want, and I want the best." Thus, I organically have less of whatever it is. The scarcity mentality has left me, and my

weight has finally, for the first time in my life, held steady at my body's happy point.

» I accept my limitations and no longer hold myself to unreasonable standards. This doesn't mean I don't push myself. It means I don't ask the impossible of myself and allow myself grace with learning curves, timeframes, and outcomes. I feel free.

» I give myself permission to be flawed, make mistakes, and say no to things without guilt. I used to hate saying no because I was valuing the other person's experience more than my own. Now, I choose myself, my own experience, and am saying yes more organically, rather than doing stuff I don't genuinely resonate with.

» My willingness to try new things has opened so many new doors to new relationships and new opportunities. I've become the person that says "yes" to trying almost anything, and I'm having so much more fun in my life, making new friends, and living bigger.

» I no longer compare myself to others and feel inadequate. I stopped perceiving that others had some sort of magic I didn't. I finally *got it*: we all have magic, and the variety is the sparkle. I love that I'm different than every other human being, and I genuinely enjoy quality time with myself. Silence is even sweeter.

» I am patient and accepting of myself, which

has created patience and acceptance of others, loving them for who they are, not who I believe they should or could be. Once upon a time, I used to be a very judgmental person, thinking that's how people would like me (wrong, it's not). I became accepting and kind toward others, and I give off more authentic love.

» My marriage is better because I feel peace within, and it organically radiates to my husband. I'm calmer, happier, and I don't bug him about all the stupid stuff I thought was important before. I'm much more easy-going and let him live his life, while I focus on mine.

» All of my relationships have improved, people notice my more positive energy and love it. I show up better and with greater truth. It has been a game-changer. My relationships have deepened.

Now, imagine the possibilities for what you can create for yourself. Take a moment right now and visualize what your life would be like if you were to make the small (and yet massive!) adjustment of being kinder to yourself. How would it affect you positively? How do you think your attitudes towards yourself and your capabilities may change? Do you feel that kindness towards yourself might improve any of the relationships you hold most dear? Dive in with the workbook at thesixhabits.com/resources.

Some specific areas to look for regarding kindness to yourself include:

» What you say to yourself about your performance or capabilities.

» What you say to yourself when you look in the mirror.

» What you say to yourself about what you eat and the excuses you make about being healthy.

KINDNESS TO OTHERS

It's often much easier to be kinder to others than it is to be kind to ourselves. Simply put, we often hold others in higher regard than we do ourselves. Being kind to others is included in this book (that aims to help *you* feel happy) because kindness to others directly benefits *us*. Our relationships improve, we enjoy our relationships more, others enjoy our company more, they're more willing to do things for us, and they're more likely to accept us as we are.

Kindness goes beyond just being nice to other people. Anybody can be nice. This isn't about nice—this is about kindness. Kindness might show up as empathy or forgiveness. It also might show up as greater generosity. Or perhaps willingness to help a stranger. When you read through the goodness chapter, you'll see a whole bunch of things that will make you feel good, that are all about being kind to others. Kindness to others is actually an incredibly selfish act, as is forgiveness. Surprise! When you are kind to others, you receive great reward in the way you feel. Often you get a surge of "warm and fuzzies," or "WAF," as I like to call that super happy feeling in your soul. I live for that feeling. It's addictive.

I want to talk about two very important subjects when it comes to kindness to others: forgiveness and honesty. I don't need to go on and on about being generous or doing acts of kindness. I think you have enough context just from being alive to fill in the blanks with those on your own. Of course, dig into the goodness chapter when you get to it for a few helpful thoughts in that area.

FORGIVENESS

I firmly believe that forgiveness is an incredibly selfish act and a beautiful one. When you forgive someone else for something they have done or something they made you feel, you are letting the feelings of anger, hurt, and resentment go. You no longer carry the burden of the incident that caused you pain.

I'll be the first one to tell you forgiveness can be very difficult. Forgiveness is not something that I showed up in life knowing how to do. It is a skill that is learned and practiced over time, just like anything else.

One of the biggest things in my life I had to forgive (for my own benefit), was the abuse I endured in my first serious relationship. I was physically assaulted, sexually abused, and verbally attacked on a daily basis. I was humiliated in front of others. I was chastised and treated like a diseased outcast. I was made fun of. What I went through sucks for anyone, and I know that so many have experienced dramatically worse.

Forgiveness when you've been victimized, regardless of what happened, is for *your* benefit. I know this might seem crazy, but bear with me.

When I left that relationship, I was broken. I couldn't stop crying. As I shared earlier, I remember staying at my parents' house with nowhere else to go, sleeping in my mom's bed and then waking up just so I could stare at the wall for hours on end. I was beyond depressed—I was disabled. I couldn't understand how I allowed such a thing to happen to myself, or why someone would ever treat me so poorly when all I had ever done was be kind to him. Every organ ached with grief. It was a remarkably low point for me, one that I have thankfully never known since.

In my time staring at the wall, I replayed all the terrible things he did to me. I speculated how a monster like that could be created, and then on the origin of everything that made him who he was. I thought about his life choices that led him to be the person he was, and I thought about the things he went through that were not his choice. It helped me to empathize and see him less as a monster, and more of a deeply damaged person doing the one thing he learned how to do from others.

I was far from forgiveness. I don't remember the exact day or the exact circumstances, but I do remember my thought. I was staring at the wall (again) and realized the only way out of my personal hell was to forgive. I tried and failed. I tried again and continued to fail. I could not get over what he did to me. I was failing because at that time, I misunderstood forgiveness. I thought it meant I had to "let it go," "let him off the hook," and thought I had to be okay with what he had done to me. I was still in so much pain, and so deeply hurt that I couldn't see the truth. I hated myself, as he had so clearly hated me.

Nevertheless, I refused to give up. The more I tried to forgive, the more I came to correctly understand that forgiveness is not letting someone "off the hook," condoning what they did, or "letting it go." Forgiveness meant releasing it and refusing to carry the burden of the pain any longer.

I remember my mother telling me when I was growing up that you must forgive and forget. I never understood the forgetting part. I always felt that you learned from the things that happened to you and you shouldn't forget them, so you wouldn't let them happen again. But as I've become older, I've come to finally understand that forgiving is release, and changing how you *feel* about what happened. Forgetting means no longer torturing yourself or the other person for something that happened in the past.

Being able to forgive this man took extraordinary effort on my part, but I did, and to this day, I still greatly benefit. It took me a long time, and in fact, I believe this abuse and the subsequent forgiveness made a substantial impact on who I have become as a person. You might be surprised to learn this, but *I'm grateful for everything I endured because I am a stronger, better, kinder person after what that situation brought out in me. I wouldn't change a thing. Really.*

One day, several years later, this man called me out of the blue. He called me to see how I was doing, and to apologize for what he had done to me. He freely admitted that he had treated me horribly and he was ashamed of himself. He asked for my forgiveness. I actually laughed with joy in my heart and genuine appreciation for the moment when I could say to him in all sincerity and love, "I don't need to, I forgave you years ago!" Like you might experience in a movie, there was a long awkward silence on the other end of the phone while he processed what I said. This man didn't feel worthy of my forgiveness, but dared to ask for it anyway, only to learn that he had been granted forgiveness years ago. I felt the joy of being able to forgive someone who deeply hurt me, and I was grateful for the opportunity to tell him (one that we don't always get).

I know now, only because of that phone call, that he had been carrying the burden of his actions on his heart for many years. He had not forgiven himself for what he had done. I would've been carrying the burden of his actions for many years too if I hadn't forgiven him. I would have been bitter, angry, and an unpleasant person. When I left that relationship and I chose to forgive him, *I became free.* My heart was lighter, and I was able to move on with my life in a way that led me to a place of actual joy and abundance. Imagine my life if I had chosen to hang onto the pain? My choice to forgive was the gift I gave to *me*.

Your choice to forgive is the gift you need to give to *you*. A handy workbook to help you dive into this is on thesixhabits. com/resources. Benefiting from forgiveness begins by truly owning what forgiveness is and understanding what it's not. Ask yourself who you need to forgive, why, and what *you* get out of it.

HONESTY

Honesty is a tricky subject—one you might think you're already good at. While you are probably already a *mostly* honest person, I know too many people who struggle with total honesty because they're afraid of consequence, someone's reaction, hurting someone, or the simple awkwardness of speaking the truth. From that perspective, you might see some areas in which you aren't as honest as you could be (yet). Examples include telling someone, "we'll see" when you actually mean "no," telling someone that they look nice when they don't, or letting your boss think you're happy when you're not. These are all examples of the common crimes against honesty we commit all the time. They *hurt ourselves and others*, limiting our potential for the best relationships with those around us.

For some reason, our culture suggests that being honest is bad, and vulnerability is a danger zone. Look at magazines and their airbrushed cover models, the news and the intense hyperbole around headlines, politicians and their exaggerated claims, our unwillingness to speak our truth when someone else might not like it, and our own head trash around what *is* happening versus what we *perceive* is happening. Our culture practically screams that being honest doesn't sell, people don't want it, it hurts other people's feelings, being honest is mean, being honest gets you in trouble, and being honest is something you should avoid because people will reject you if they hear it. This is what our society and culture have reinforced, and many of us believe and practice this every day. It's not healthy. It leads to disingenuous relationships with ourselves and with others. These relationships end up being built on flimsy lies that can't withstand actual pressure.

The best relationships I have are the ones that are totally honest. I hate the phrase "brutally honest" because it implies honesty is brutal when it doesn't have to be. The package that honesty comes in is a choice—you always have the option to *choose* to be gentle or brutal. Your discomfort with the truth, or with the potential reaction often flavors the wrapping you default to and gives you the illusion that you don't have a choice. Much like the wrapping paper you choose for a gift, how you wrap the truth is your choice. You're free to do it how you like, and you can choose something lovely then wrap it with care. I feel like I can probably write an entire book about the subject of honesty (and I may do it someday) and how to lovingly be honest with others. Instead, I'll give you three relatable examples of how not being fully honest with others is unkind because it's actually hurting them and you.

At the end of each of the three examples, there are questions to help you identify your honesty patterns as they exist now and what could be possible through changing them. I'll ask you to think about things from both the perspectives: the one withholding the honesty, and the one not receiving it. There's a workbook available on thesixhabits.com/resources if you want some guided help with this subject.

Example 1: "I want to avoid discomfort."

Think of one of your best friends, the one that loves to throw the occasional party. Imagine that he invites you to a party, and he's collecting responses. You don't want to go, but you don't want to hurt his feelings either, so you don't respond for weeks. You think you might be able to talk yourself into going, but you're an introvert, and even though you sincerely love your friend, you just don't want to go. It has nothing to do with him, and everything to do with you. However, you're still worried about hurting his feelings and making him feel bad. At the same time, you're avoiding making a clear decision, delivering it, and feeling your own personal discomfort.

What you don't realize on the other side of things, is that your friend *does* need the RSVP because he is trying to figure out exactly how much food and alcohol to purchase, and he's running out of time to shop. Your response matters (as does your presence in his life), not because he wants to change your mind, not because he wants to guilt you into going, or because he doesn't understand you're an introvert that absolutely hates parties, but because he needs to plan. So, as the weeks pass by and the party draws ever nearer, *you still don't respond.*

You see your friend for coffee, and he asks you if you're going to come or not, and you respond, "We'll see. I don't know yet." The disingenuous part is that you *do* know, but just don't want to say what you know already out of fear for his reaction. "We'll see" is a cop-out, and it's what frustrated parents say to their children when they won't stop nagging them. By refusing to answer your friend with your truth, you rob him of the respect he deserves as an adult and the credit for being an adult who can handle hearing your genuine response.

If you're worried about his feelings, and you're afraid of a poor outcome, work on the delivery and take the leap of faith into honesty. This is an investment in *strengthening* the relationship, not weakening it. You could say instead, "I genuinely love that you invited me and want me to celebrate with you, but parties give me anxiety. I love spending one-on-one time with you and I enjoy our conversations, though. I'm going to decline to come to the party but would love to do something else with you instead. I hope you understand how I feel, and we can plan something else that works for both of us."

In all likelihood, he won't be upset with you for telling him how you feel in such a loving, caring and respectful way. After all, you're not rejecting him or insulting him. If anything, you're reaffirming how much you care about him and enjoy the friendship. You're even taking the time to explain your feelings. Few people do this, so having this level of graceful honesty will be shocking *and* delightful. How do I know? I've used the ultra-honesty approach time and time again. Not once has anyone ever become upset with me. In fact, many people have told me how much they get it, how relatable my thoughts are, and that they're excited to do something one on one with me.

This particular issue of the RSVP is quite common. Have you ever been the inviter who waits and waits for answers? Have you ever been the reluctant invitee who just can't give an answer? How do you think you could do better next time?

Example 2: "I don't want to hurt their feelings."

Think of another one of your friends, the one that's going after some new, big, shiny accomplishment in their career. Imagine she's getting ready, and she asks you how she looks. She happens to be wearing a dress that's hideous and makes her butt look like the back end of a bus. She's going to a business event, looking for investors and first impressions critically matter at this event. She needs to look chic, polished, and like a power player. Unfortunately, the outfit she has on is something she *thought* might look OK, but isn't actually appropriate for the occasion, and isn't flattering on her. She looks sloppy, and you don't want to tell her because you don't want to hurt her feelings. You want to avoid an uncomfortable conversation. So, you say *nothing*.

Skip ahead, and she goes to the event. People make silent judgments about her (whether they should or should not is irrelevant right now), and she can't understand why people don't take her seriously. She's confused, and she comes home from the event feeling defeated, and wondering what she said or did that made people not take her seriously. She thought it might've been her outfit, but since you reassured her, she dismissed the thought. She spends days trying to pick apart every moment and wondering what she could have possibly done better. Meanwhile, if you had just told her the truth, you would've saved her from blowing it and second-guessing herself for days.

You don't have to say something horrible like, "That looks terrible on you, go change." You can't say that to most people. People can barely handle all of the bullying they dish out at themselves, never mind bullying coming from someone they love. A nice way to tell her the truth in that moment would be, "I know how important this event is to you, and I want to make sure you feel super powerful in the outfit you've chosen. If you're asking for my opinion right now it means you have some doubt. Maybe you should go back in your closet and find the power outfit you *know* without question makes you feel as powerful as you need to feel to crush this event."

In this example, as in the last one, accurate information, and the presentation of the information is what separates bad truth from good truth, making all the difference. Have I used this too? Many times. The key here has always been to point out the doubt within the person I love for the decision they're about to make, so they can see it themselves and make a better choice on their own. Nine times out of ten, it works very well. When it doesn't? I try some version of this instead: "I love you, so I'm going to give you my opinion from a place of love and fully advocating for your success. This is not your "power" look, and I would advise that you change into something else. I worry this is compromising the impression you're trying to make. I apologize if this hurts, but you did ask me, and I want to love you enough to give you the truth you've asked for. I can help you pick something else if you want."

While that hasn't always been met with a smile, the result has always been met with gratitude and love. I decided a long time ago that I'm strong enough to be honest and love my friends and family *better*, the way they deserve. Whenever

I've had to give potentially hurtful honesty, I gave my loved ones the gift of truth, and wrapped it with all of the gentle love I had, along with my rationale. You can too.

Have you ever doubted yourself and needed someone to have your back by making sure you looked your best? Have you ever been asked by someone you love what you thought of their presentation, their outfit, their proposal, or something they've worked hard on? Do you think someone might be upset with you for withholding the truth? In what ways do you think you can do better next time?

Example 3: "I don't want to get in trouble."

In this final example, I want to talk about work, but there are many similarities to be found between this professional example and some of the more intimate relationships in our lives that could benefit from telling the truth earlier, clearer, or at all.

Once upon a time, I had an incredibly bright, charming, and energetic young lady on my staff. I felt very lucky to have her work for me. She always brought a fantastic energy to the working environment and constantly made me laugh. She did excellent work, the clients liked her, and she always had a smile on her face. Unfortunately, because she was afraid of my reaction (fearing I would punish her somehow), and how I might feel personally rejected, she never told me how unhappy she was feeling at work while I still had the chance to do something about it. She had built it up in her head to be this big massive problem worse than death.

When she finally did tell me, I learned that due to a

confluence of issues, she fell out of love with the job itself, she fell out of love with the entire field, and she didn't appreciate how some of the clients made her feel sometimes. Because she never told me or her direct manager how she felt, we could never address the problem for her or correct it. I could never fix how she felt about the clients. I could never give her an opportunity to try a different job within the company. I couldn't give her some well-earned time off. I couldn't listen and just let her get it off her chest—I couldn't do anything.

I valued this young lady greatly. I was grateful to have her be a part of my life and a part of my company. She was (and is) that fantastic. I appreciated everything about her and told her frequently. However, because of her decision to *not* tell me how she truly felt, she did us both a disservice. She wasn't honest with me about how she felt, and she didn't trust me to respond to her genuine feelings with kindness, empathy, and understanding. As a result, she endured months of frustration and many days of silent suffering in a job she used to love, which ultimately led to her leaving my company as the truth came tumbling out one day amidst heart palpitations, a flood of tears, and deep frustration when the dam finally burst. She couldn't take it anymore.

My heart sank when she told me she was leaving and why. I felt guilty for not knowing what was going on (and not fixing it when I could have). I wondered what I could've possibly done to have changed her experience to be something better and prayed that there was still the chance. I asked her if there was anything I could do to keep her, and she said no. She never allowed me to address the problem. People can't fix problems they can't see. It was a loss for both of us.

She has since learned from the experience. She went on to explore other things, make different choices about honesty and disclosure in subsequent situations, and is doing well in life. The lesson she learned was a painful but powerful one, but the experience served its purpose.

In this example, the disclosure of the truth of her feelings would have made a tremendous difference for her quality of life, satisfaction in her career, and my ability to help her work through the things she could control on her own. This was less about the "how," unlike the other two examples, and more about the great importance and impact of honesty.

In your relationship with the one(s) you love, how are you withholding your feelings and "putting up with" something out of fear of their reaction? In your career, how are you withholding your frustrations and not helping to co-create solutions to address the things that bother you? Where in your life does this apply to you, and what do you stand to gain from speaking your truth?

REDIRECTION

Have you ever seen the chalk street art that looks like an incredible optical illusion of a giant hole in the sidewalk? (It's so cool. Google "Julian Beever" or "Manfred Stader" to see it if you haven't.) The artist creates a chalk drawing with incredible detail that when viewed from the right angle, looks like the real deal. From every other angle, it looks like a chalk drawing, except it's distorted. The drawing is meant to encourage you to look at things from the right perspective to get the ideal view. While I have no idea how those artists create such incredible perspective on the pavement, I *do* know how people encourage themselves to look at things from the right perspective to get the ideal view of themselves, others, and life in general.

Redirection plays a pivotal role in our successes, especially in relation to kindness and acceptance. Kindness and acceptance go hand in hand, and redirection is the glue keeping them together. As much as I would love it if you were to read these pages, have the light bulb go on, and suddenly be all better, we both know that's not happening. In order to become kinder to yourself and others, the work you need to do comes with a heavy helping of redirection. Kindness takes practice, and there are three important steps to take every time you start with negativity.

Before we dive in, I want to invite you to download the workbook I created to help you with this section. Get it at thesixhabits.com/resources. You may wish to print that out and have it handy *before* you go further.

DESTRUCTIVE → INSTRUCTIVE → CONSTRUCTIVE

A *destructive* thought, word, or action is one that destroys. This is the voice of the bully. It's damaging, it tears a person down, it's negative, and it's not helpful at all. Think of when you're bullying yourself. You say mean things to yourself and they're destructive to your self-esteem, happiness, and confidence. Destruction is the opposite of construction.

An *instructive* thought, word, or action is one that teaches, informs, and advocates. This is the voice of the teacher and the inner coach. It's useful, educational, enlightening and it directs why and how we build (or construct). Think of the last time you learned something new, either in a classroom setting or on your own. You were most likely objective and unemotional about it, simply absorbing new information and context around instructions. You also absorbed powerful rationale as to *why* you should apply that knowledge, and how to do whatever it was you were learning.

A *constructive* thought, word, or action is one that builds. This is the voice of the nurturing parent. It's helpful, productive, and a useful tool that can move mountains. Think of how you feel when someone says something nice about you, how that builds you up, and gives you a little bounce in your step. Using constructive thoughts, words, or actions takes the chains off your potential and gives you the freedom and genuine power to do anything you want.

THE 1-2-3 KNOCKOUT

The redirecting process with your thoughts and speech begins with identifying the *destructive* narrative you use with yourself and others. From there, you must be *instructive* with your mind and express leadership over the narrative by intentionally stating (in thought or speech) the benefit of redirection. You must also identify why your destructive narrative needs redirection. Finally, you must restate the negative narrative into a *constructive* one, even if you don't genuinely believe it yet. Think of it as telling the truth in advance.

An important note for you: constructive thoughts are not necessarily affirmations. While constructive thoughts can be affirmations, they are often just simple, helpful, constructive thoughts.

Here are some examples of destructive things that we will build upon to teach you the 1-2-3 Knockout:

> » Destructive: I hate the way I look.

> » Destructive: I'm not very good at this.

> » Destructive: I will never forgive that jerk for what he did to me.

> » Destructive: I could never start a business. I don't know where to begin.

> » Destructive: I'm weak, I can't work out.

> » Destructive: I don't want to make this call. It's going to go badly.

STOPPING THE DESTRUCTION

We can hear our negative internal and external monologues. We *know* when we're saying all the wrong things. We know it deep down in our bones, but we don't do anything about it. We accept what we say as how we think and speak. We think there isn't any other way—it's just how we live our lives.

I have great news for you. Because you already hear yourself, even if it's just some of the time, you're already thirty-three percent there! Hearing yourself means you're on the way to permanently redirecting your thoughts and speech to a more constructive narrative that will support you and help you be the person you most wish to be.

No one can fix a problem they aren't aware of. The important difference between passively hearing it and doing something about it is actively hearing it, identifying it, and calling it out.

Your monologue might sound like mine, where you catch yourself and actually talk to yourself. Either out loud or in my head, I unabashedly talk to myself all the time when I'm getting ready for the day, driving in the car, at work, in a meeting, etc. I've always said mean stuff to myself, and sometimes still do, but I've become a ninja at redirecting myself. The mean stuff is slowing to a meager trickle. You can expect the same gradual decrease in your own journey, and one day we'll both be kind to ourselves one hundred percent.

I want you to remember that the instructive voice is the voice of the teacher and the advocate. Here are some of the instructional comments I've said to myself after catching myself in a destructive moment. Maybe you'll recognize your own thoughts. I really want you to notice that these are not constructive thoughts. They're not meant to be. These comments are the voice of reason, critique, and advocacy. These are the bridging comments that remind you to stop being destructive, and why.

> » Woah! That wasn't nice.

> » Why are you being such a jerk to yourself? You wouldn't say that to your friends.

> » That's wrong and you know it. Cut it out.

> » Damn girl—WTF?

> » Ouch! Try again!

> » You're better than this. Stop it.

> » You're not going to reach your goals if you keep talking to yourself like that!

These are great examples of some of the things we say to someone else who might be mean to themselves, right? Take this as your cue to love yourself harder and remind yourself that what you're doing is hurtful. If you don't love yourself today, that's okay— you're learning, and your inner coach has your back. Catch yourself, talk to yourself, and state that what you're thinking, saying, or doing is unacceptable. Then you can move on with some power!

GIVING OURSELVES INSTRUCTION

Now that you've caught yourself, you need to teach and remind yourself. Teaching yourself might be a little difficult at first, but with practice, you'll be able to give yourself pretty impressive marching orders a lot faster than you think.

Start with your "why." Your "why" is your powerful reason to redirect. Maybe you're telling yourself you hate the way you look. Why do you want to redirect? Other than being a terrible thought, you want to ask yourself how you will benefit from doing something better. Maybe you stand to gain better self-esteem if you learn to like the way you look. Perhaps you'll have better energy others will want to be around. Maybe it's so you can be a better role model for your children. Whatever your "why" is, use that as a starting point. Follow the thought process using the destructive thoughts above, but adding in the instructive, in a style of advocacy and reason.

> » Destructive: I hate the way I look.

> » Instructive: I want to love the way I look, and if I constantly tear myself down, I'll never get there. I've got to stop.

> » Destructive: I'm not very good at this.

> » Instructive: I'm learning, and everyone starts somewhere. I can do this, and I need to pump myself up so I can do it.

> » Destructive: I will never forgive that jerk for what he did to me.

> » Instructive: I am learning to forgive, and it takes practice. I can forgive, and I will. For today, I am doing my best and making progress.

» Destructive: I could never start a business. I don't know where to begin.

» Instructive: I can learn, and I need to cheer myself on.

» Destructive: I'm weak, I can't work out.

» Instructive: No one is strong when they start, and that's okay.

» Destructive: I don't want to make this call. It's going to go badly.

» Instructive: I can make this call, and I'll get better and better with every call I make.

You need to use everything you know about why your destructive thoughts, words, and actions are bad. You have to understand how they're hurting you, what you stand to gain by changing, and ultimately, your "why," to help reframe your thinking. After you do this for a few weeks, you will develop proficiency, and you won't need to go through this entire process every time. It *will* become automatic, it *will* become easy, and you'll default to instructive thinking as soon as you catch yourself.

STARTING THE CONSTRUCTION

This is the fun part, and this is what could be considered "telling the truth in advance." If you don't automatically think good thoughts about yourself already, you're stuck in the habit of negativity, and you're not going to come out of the gate believing the new constructive thoughts just because I told you to. However, the more frequently you tell yourself the new constructive things, the longer you do it, and the better you get at it, the more you will start to believe the new constructive things. They will become your *new truth*.

You didn't pick up this book so you could continue the same destructive habits and feeling the exact same way. "I'm telling the truth in advance" is your new mantra. I promise you're going to need it when you feel silly for saying things you do not believe (yet). If you don't have the mantra you can repeat in your head as often as possible, you're going to feel stupid, you're going to second-guess yourself, and you're not going to do the work because the little bully inside your head that loves to spew mean things from the megaphone of your mind is hard at work. You've had your whole life to get insanely, over-the-top, blazingly good at being unkind to yourself and others. Do you really think that unlearning that is going to be a simple "Ah-ha" moment, and then you're all better? At this point in the book, we both know better. We're real with each other now. No lies, no fluff.

So how exactly do you start the construction? Generally, the easiest most obvious way is to start with the exact opposite of the destruction:

» Destructive: I *hate* the way I look.

» Instructive: I want to love the way I look, and if I constantly tear myself down, I'll never get there. I've got to stop.

» Constructive: I *love* the way I look.

» Destructive: I *don't want* to make this call. It's going to go *badly*.

» Instructive: I can make this call, and I'll get better and better with every call I make.

» Constructive: I *want* to make this call. It's going to go *well*.

If that feels awkward or ill-fitting, restate that you're becoming, working on, learning to, growing in, getting better at, and so on:

» Destructive: I'm *not* very good at this.

» Instructive: I'm learning, and everyone starts somewhere. I can do this, and I need to pump myself up so I *can* do it.

» Constructive: I am *becoming* good at this.

» Destructive: I'm *weak*, I *can't* work out.

» Instructive: No one is strong when they start, and that's ok.

» Constructive: I'm *becoming* strong, and I *can*

work out.

If that doesn't quite fit either, use "I am" language to give proper framing to new thoughts, words, or actions that you're either working on or considering cultivating.

> » Destructive: I will *never* forgive that jerk for what he did to me.

> » Instructive: I am learning to forgive, and it takes practice. I can forgive, and I will. For today, I am doing my best and making progress.

> » Constructive: *I am* forgiving him.

> » Destructive: I could *never* start a business. I *don't know* where to begin.

> » Instructive: I can learn, and I need to cheer myself on.

> » Constructive: I am starting a business. I *will find out* where to begin.

Whatever redirection language you give yourself, make sure it's encouraging the good and helping to reinforce construction. If you take nothing else from this section, remember three little words:

> » Destruction

> » Instruction

> » Construction

You might get so good at instruction that you go from

deconstructive to constructive in the blink of an eye. I did, and I know you will.

Using all the powerful information in this section, I challenge you to practice your 1-2-3 Knockout using your current destructive thoughts until you've covered all of them and the process really sinks in. You can grab a pen and practice in a notebook, you can make a 3-column table on your computer, or if you want it all laid out for you with instructions, you can download the guided workbook on thesixhabits.com/resources (if you haven't already).

To master this important skill, you will want to practice this enough so that it becomes part of your new default behavior. Allow the process to take as much time it needs to take and give yourself the grace to learn and practice without judgment.

THE BOTTOM LINE

Kindness is an essential part of happiness. Your ability to manifest all that you want to *have*, all that you want to *do* and all that you want to *be* in life depends on your kindness to yourself and others.

Kindness to yourself:

1. Starts with observation

2. Continues with redirection

3. Lasts by daily habit and construction

» A few key areas to watch for are: your career, your family, your appearance, and your goals

Kindness to others is found in many forms:

» Empathy, acts of kindness, generosity, listening, actions, and more.

» Forgiveness, which is a beneficial form of self-care.

» Honesty, which is where clear communication creates better relationships.

2. Acceptance

Acceptance is the habit governing self-love, acceptance of self, past, decisions, flaws, and the totality of being. It is the habit of accepting what is, versus rejection of self in favor of a desired alternate expression.

ACCEPTING YOURSELF

Perhaps the biggest area of struggle that some of us face is the struggle to accept ourselves. Acceptance is love in its purest form. Acceptance is how you *feel* about yourself, whereas kindness is how you *treat* yourself. Accepting who we are as people, accepting where we are in life, accepting what we look like, accepting our idiosyncrasies, accepting mistakes we've made, accepting the very core of what makes us, well, *us*, is difficult.

It doesn't help that so many things in social media, mass media, and even our own upbringing force us to compare ourselves to others and feel shame for being human. We're exposed to photos of women who are more slender and more buxom than we are (thank you, Photoshop). We're exposed to videos of men bench-pressing more weight than a small truck, images of people enjoying "the good life" we don't have, and much more. Despite the fact that many of the images have been altered or staged, they still affect us psychologically.

Our parents want the best for us, our teachers tell us we're good, bad, etc., and constantly label us in a well-meaning effort to shape us into what society tells us is a functional person (with no regard for being a *happy* person). There's only one problem. It's all a lie, and it's eating us alive.

In many ways, how you feel about yourself, and all the trappings of your life in your own personal meat suit aren't your fault. You were told a number of things that informed you how to feel about everything. You were given ideas of what beauty is. What success is. What happiness is. What sex is. And because you didn't know any better, you believed it. We all did. Don't believe me? Look on the cover of any magazine and evaluate what I said.

One of the most valuable things you can ever do for yourself is to accept yourself, as-is, with no qualifiers and no conditions. It doesn't mean you can't strive for more, or better. It means you love yourself the way you are, where you are, and for who you are. You love yourself right now, even if you are a work in progress. It means that you stop trying to put love in the distant context of "I'll love myself when," and choose to do it now instead. You're not changing yourself to be worthy of self-love, you're merely changing how you feel, and deciding you're worthy *now*—because you are.

I make zero assertions that this is an easy task. It's hard and I'm the girl who spent years wishing she didn't have freckles, wishing she didn't have cellulite, wishing she was richer, wishing she could make more sales, wishing she was more popular. Take it from me, *wishing won't get you there or change a damn thing—it will only make you feel bad about yourself.* You have to do the work to feel good and if so desired, change the things you don't like about yourself (while loving yourself the whole time). I've been doing the work almost my whole adult life, and it doesn't happen overnight. My journey has been long, fraught with frustration, self-loathing, stumbles, gym memberships, skin treatments, crash diets, get-rich-quick schemes, and much more. Many companies profited from my insecurity over the years.

I can't tell you how much I hated myself when I was a teenager. I don't know that a large enough word exists to encapsulate the enormity of the self-loathing I felt. School didn't help. They say kids are mean and they are *correct*. If you can believe it, I asked seven boys to go to senior prom with me and was rejected seven times. Yep, that hurt. I was dumped by the first boy I loved because I wouldn't have sex with him before I was ready. I struggled in half my classes and barely passed, then sailed through the other half because they made sense. The popular kids made fun of me for any reason they could think of. I was kicked around, picked on, bullied, and so much more. It wasn't pretty—I was angry, bitter, and hated myself. You get the idea. They hated me, why shouldn't I hate me? Accepting myself was not an option.

Everything I went through when I was younger made a powerful impression on my psyche. Regrettably, not a positive one. When I got into my first real adult relationship at nineteen, I found myself pregnant and in what I would quickly learn was a physically, mentally, and verbally abusive relationship. It made me feel empty and worthless. He was supposed to love me and yet, he treated me like he hated me. He constantly told me I wasn't good enough, wasn't pretty enough, and at 5'6" and 120 pounds, I was fat. He said I wasn't adventurous enough sexually and complained he "had" to be the one to take my virginity because "someone has to get it over with."

One day, when the abuse became too much to bear, I called my dad, who came to my rescue. During the thirty-minute drive it took for my dad to get from his house to mine, I'd been so beaten down mentally that I'd changed my tune to believe I deserved it and tried to talk my dad out of taking me away. I even asked my dad to let me give the jerk another chance. Again, I was angry, bitter, and hated myself. Accepting myself was laughable.

I finally left the jerk and moved on, but my struggles weren't over. I had a string of jobs, and in one year, I had fourteen jobs. No one wanted to hire me for a decent job because I didn't have enough education, enough experience, and I had a "chip on my shoulder." I was fired from half my jobs and quit the rest because of how they made me feel. I was still angry, bitter, and hating myself—only more so. Accept myself? Puh-lease.

At this point in my tender young life, I had been thoroughly rejected by what felt like everything and everyone that I *thought* I needed acceptance and approval from. Acceptance was *far* from the reach of my sad mind. I was too busy trying to survive. I finally made a powerful move away from feeling bad about myself, but only out of desperation to feel anything other than rejection and failure.

I wanted to start a company I couldn't be fired from. I didn't want to be angry or bitter anymore because it was eating me alive. I didn't want to hate myself. So, I started my first company. I worked tirelessly when I wasn't busy at other jobs to get clients, to make sales, and to figure things out. It wasn't like I had a social life to tend to. No big sacrifice there.

A family member discouraged me and told me I couldn't do it. When I insisted, she wanted to "let me" do free work for her so I could build my portfolio. Gee, how generous. I met with people who only took the meeting with me so they could pursue less noble intentions. I made sales and had people refuse to pay me. I had people outright tell me I wasn't professional enough. I had people steal my ideas and steal my clients. All before most people graduate college. *Really? Can no one cut me some slack and let me win for once?* This continued for years, and oftentimes I let it define how I felt about myself.

However, starting my company was the beginning of my journey to accepting myself, even though I didn't know it at the beginning. I started distancing myself from the voices of negativity by going on my own. I began to prove to myself that I could do things because I had no other choice but to be successful—or I wouldn't eat. Necessity may be the mother of invention, but it is also the father of relentlessness.

I worked hard to win business, get smarter, network, get referrals, make clients happy, stop people from stealing from me, demand I get paid, win legal fights, and so much more. It was all out of utter exhaustion from being treated badly and not having any other alternative. I couldn't afford to fail.

I will always love how Eminem famously rapped about failure not being an option in his song "Lose Yourself," released in 2002. When that song first came out, I was twenty-one, a young entrepreneur, and had a fire in my belly that would not be extinguished. I heard that song quite a bit in the following years and felt the inferno inside of me every time. That one lyric always stood out and still does. I refused to give up on myself.

As I was building my business, I had to learn fast. I couldn't afford to let my clients *not* pay me. I couldn't afford to be the world's doormat anymore—my bills wouldn't get paid if I did. I'd heard so many times that I couldn't do something because I wasn't smart enough, or I didn't know how to do it, or I didn't have enough money, or I didn't know the right people, *blah blah blah*. Lots of people seemed to enjoy telling me what I couldn't do and felt it was their duty to keep me small. My mantra quickly became: "Watch me." I succeeded because my will to survive and *thrive* was strong.

Through my early successes, I saw the absurdity in the things people had said about me all those years. I understood why others stole from me and why they didn't pay. It had nothing to do with me, but everything to do with their own need for survival and their own insecurities. I finally saw through all the lies I'd heard for years about my capabilities, my worth, my value, my intellect, and more. I began to feel better, but not entirely.

While you're on the journey to accepting yourself, you

must constantly fight off the "noise" of the outside world and everything anyone has ever told you about life. But first, *you have to choose it.* Yes, it's that simple—just decide to. I'm asking you to choose it for yourself. I want to take you on the journey with me. I want you to join me in the liberation and joy of self-acceptance. While I still have my days of self-loathing and second-guessing, they're pretty few and far between now. I honestly can't even remember the last time I had one; it's been that long. I genuinely like me, love me, and think I'm a pretty awesome human. I am. And I want you to feel the same way about yourself because it's *true.*

When I put myself through uncomfortable situations as a budding professional, I grew tremendously in my capabilities and my self-esteem because despite all my losses, I had a lot of wins. I proved to myself that I'm not a worthless loser. I did the work. Honestly, I put myself through hell. When I purposefully decided to love myself, it took a great deal of deciding every day to accept all of myself: my failures along with my wins, my appearance, including my freckles, my slim self, including all that cellulite, my lazy mistakes alongside my wholehearted victorious journeys, my heart's beauty and ugliness—all of it. Essentially, I had to accept my humanity. The hardest part was reminding myself to choose acceptance every day. I'll be honest and tell you I didn't always remind myself, but most days I did. It made the difference. I decided to talk things out with a therapist for years. I did hours of journaling, typed my fingers off, and repeated affirmations until I felt like Stuart Smalley (please, I beg you to look it up on YouTube). I did the work that felt hokey, and darn it, it worked. I got there. You will too. ***You will be a happier,*** *infinitely more daring, courageous, and capable person when you choose to do the work to accept and love yourself. It's virtually guaranteed.*

ACCEPTING OTHERS

One of the major challenges we face in our relationships is expectations. It goes like this: we meet others, we enter some type of relationship, and we have expectations of how that person is going to behave, treat us, and communicate. All types of relationships break down (including love, friendship, family and business) when those expectations go unmet. They go unmet because often the expectations are unreasonable, not communicated, or just plain unfair.

We fail to understand that the other people we're in a relationship with have their own set of complex backstories, feelings, insecurities, limitations, and thoughts. None of those things are about us at all. The way people treat us is more about them, their life story, what they've been through, how they were raised, how they feel about the world, how they feel about themselves, what they like, what they dislike, etc.

Accepting others is easier than accepting ourselves but can still be difficult. You can't change other people. Only they can change themselves. We all have to want to change on our own.

The joy and freedom in accepting others come from loving these people because of who they really are, not in spite of it. Here's a real example that countless people might identify with:

A woman is in a marriage that leaves her unfulfilled, and joyless. Her husband is a sedentary, video-game loving, smart man who loves nothing more than staying home and working the bare minimum to keep the lights on. For him, that's his definition of time well-spent and a life well-lived. This woman's definition differs greatly, and she emphatically insists he has a great deal of potential and could do much more. She clings to the hope that he will rise to his potential and do things *her* way. However, despite multiple threats of divorce, he is still who he is and still makes the same choices time after time.

This woman is choosing unhappiness, and the problematic aspect is that she stays married to him for who he *could* be, not for who he *is*. She's miserable and unfulfilled as a result (and so is he!). Her unhappiness comes from not accepting her husband and loving him for who he is. He has always been this way and has never represented himself to be any other way. Is he wrong for not fulfilling his potential? Is she wrong for expecting him to change when he clearly doesn't want to?

Happiness for this woman will be found in the moment she decides to powerfully choose to love her husband for who he actually is—not in spite of it. When (and if) she decides to accept him for who he is, she may decide she doesn't want that life, and that's okay. She may also decide she can live with him, as he is, and be happy—and that's okay too. Ultimately, she cannot change him. The only thing this woman can change is how she feels about the situation and her reaction to it. Nothing more, nothing less. It will make all the difference to her enjoyment of the marriage (or desire to leave it), her husband's enjoyment of the marriage, and the marriage's chances of survival.

Accepting others begins by observing who they really are and the choices they make on their own. From there, you must give up the illusion of control in the situation. Not sure which way to go? Ask yourself if you:

> » *can* accept the situation the way it is and choose to be happy

OR

> » *cannot* accept the situation, and what you're willing to do about it (e.g. remove yourself)

The only answer that isn't fair to you or the other person is constantly trying to control or change them because of your own refusal to accept who they are, the choices they make, and the way they want to live their life.

Here's your test to determine if you need to accept someone else and/or their behavior:

> » Has the other person agreed to meet your expectations?

> » Are your expectations reasonable and fair from *their* point of view?

> » Can you change the current situation by your efforts alone?

If you're answering "no" to the questions, you might need to accept what is. If you're answering "yes," you may be in a position to change what's going on and *should*. Remember: You're not changing the other person when you accept them. You're only changing how you *feel* about them and the choices they make.

Download the workbook from thesixhabits.com/resources to help you do a deep dive here and really lean into accepting others.

EMPATHY

Empathy is a part of acceptance that will help you enjoy your *own* life more. It's widely defined as understanding someone else's feelings through *their* frame of reference.

When we don't accept others for who they are or how they're showing up, it takes a toll on us. It can manifest in controlling behaviors, anxiety, codependency, and self-destructive behaviors. Accepting *yourself* is about love and how you regard yourself. Accepting *others* is also about love and letting them be *who* they are, *how* they are, *as* they are—while living your life on your own terms. Sometimes people behave in ways we don't like or understand, have annoying habits, or can't keep their promises. Sometimes people just do things we can't and won't understand. It's not our job to do so.

Your primary job in life is to take care of *you*. Taking care of you means that you don't carry things that aren't yours to carry.

Throughout life, we intersect with others on their journeys. We get along effortlessly with a select few, and these people can develop into the closest relationships we have. Think close family, good friends, and significant others. Let's call these our "Inner Circle."

With most of the world, intimacy isn't part of the relationship we share, but we interact anyway. Think co-workers, family, acquaintances, clients, and bosses. Let's call these our "Outer Circle."

Finally, there are the people we just don't click with, and they don't have much of a place in our lives, if any at all. Think estranged family, exes, co-workers we don't click with, bosses we don't like, rude people, etc. Let's call these "Everyone Else."

With our Inner Circle, empathy typically comes naturally to us. When our best friend is unusually aggressive, we can often instinctively understand we're not the cause, and something else must be bugging them. So, we ask. We ask to get in their world and understand their feelings from their frame of reference. We learn, we understand, and we empathize. Through empathy, we deepen our relationship and strengthen the bond. We are able to accept our friend's behavior even if we don't like or tolerate it because we can clearly see the reason.

When our children are sad, we automatically ask what happened to upset them. We learn more, can understand, and are given an opportunity to help by soothing and offering kind words. We build a stronger relationship with our children by considering their feelings from *their* worldview, which might not be one we'd instinctively understand, but perhaps at one point, we did. Through our empathy, we demonstrate love and compassion. We are able to accept our child's behavior even if we don't like or tolerate it because we can clearly see the reason.

With our Outer Circle, empathy can still come naturally, but we usually suppress it, feeling as though it's inappropriate. We often subconsciously feel empathy is reserved for intimate relationships and that's where it lives, period. Relationships in the Outer Circle, while good, are *not* intimate, and we perceive they may contain land mines we're afraid to step on. If something is happening in one of these relationships, we might feel it's intrusive, invasive, or inappropriate to seek out the information needed to offer empathy and understanding.

For example, when a co-worker has a bad day, it's easy to ignore. Wrongly, our society teaches us to avoid discomfort and that vulnerability exposes us to being hurt by others. "Mind your business," people say, and we heed the advice. We don't ask people to become vulnerable, and we don't offer our own vulnerability either. The price we pay is a lack of intimacy.

While I don't expect to change *the* world, I aim to help *you* change *your* world. I advocate for leaning into the discomfort with our Outer Circle and asking the empathic questions to understand for their benefit, as well as ours. However, I also know sometimes it's not appropriate (think hostile boss). In those moments, empathy becomes an act of acceptance, not to be confused with tolerance, that benefits *us*.

With the Outer Circle, empathy can be a little gray and murky. However, with Everyone Else, empathy is clearer and becomes an act of acceptance that *benefits* us. Empathy informs how we behave with Everyone Else as well as the Outer Circle.

Let's say you're in a grocery store check-out line and all is well. You're up next, and the conveyer belt is loaded with your items, inching toward the register. The cashier scans the items slowly and systematically, bagging items for you with care. Midway through your transaction, and with your belt still loaded with items, another customer comes up behind you and starts slamming their items down on the belt. They bang the divider down with a huff. Once all their items are on the belt, they glare at the cashier and make under-the-breath comments about how slow the cashier is. Soon enough, their comments become extremely rude and loud. The longer the cashier takes, the more the customer gets visibly agitated. They become so irate they start barking at the cashier to move faster and hurry up.

The now-stressed-out and humiliated cashier mumbles an apology, continues to move at the same pace, and finishes your order amidst glares from the other customer. You leave, upset. The cashier checks out the irate customer and finishes out their day at work, also upset. However, it is the angry customer who is most upset, having started out miserable, and ending up infuriated.

In this example, we see three things. First, you are the observer. Second, the cashier is a trigger for the customer.

Third, the other customer is representative of "Everyone Else." Putting it all together, here's what we know. The customer just got triggered, the cashier is now being abused, and you as the observer, are most likely horrified by this person's behavior. Maybe you say something, maybe you don't. But, either way, you're upset.

What we don't see is the prior, *hidden* trigger. The hidden trigger is what happened to the other customer beforehand— the thing *you didn't see* that made them enter your life and the cashier's life so aggressively. In the famous bullfights of Spain, the bull isn't angry before the main event. The bull is usually calmly munching on his hay, living life, and then is triggered and injured to provoke a reaction. The trigger makes him behave the way you see on TV and in movies. A bull that hasn't been triggered isn't interesting, doesn't want to fight, and isn't upset. A random customer in a grocery store that hasn't been triggered isn't upset either.

With the Inner Circle, we will *typically* and automatically ask what's going on so we can understand and empathize. We can comfortably seek out the reason for the behavior, even if we can't tolerate it because we have the context of a safe relationship in which to contain the inquiry. By contrast, while we have *good* relationships with the Outer Circle, we don't have the context of a safe relationship to contain any inquiry. It's risky and confusing. So, we will *sometimes* ask what's going on so we can understand and empathize, and sometimes we won't. While we should do it at every opportunity for our benefit and the other person's, that's not always welcome or practical. Many times, we are left to sort it out in our heads, just get over it, or make decisions about what we will and won't tolerate—then take action accordingly.

When we get to Everyone Else, believe it or not, empathy actually gets *easier* because there's no gray, murky area to contend with. While you could inquire (some of us do), ninety-nine percent of the time you're not going to ask the irate customer in the grocery store what's going on in their day so you can understand their behavior. You can, however, assume they have a reason, and accept that you *won't* know what it is. Maybe it's a mental illness. Maybe they just got off the phone with their doctor and they found out they have cancer. Maybe they're in the middle of a custody battle with their ex. Or just got fired. Or they're in severe pain. The reason doesn't matter.

Your job isn't to know the reason. Your job is to *understand that a reason exists* and offer compassion (and love) to that person silently. This is acceptance, and this benefits you. You're accepting what happens. I want to be crystal clear about this: this doesn't mean you condone their behavior. It simply means you accept it for what it is then release it from your mind and your day. You don't allow yourself to take it personally, you don't allow yourself to make it mean more than what it does. Acceptance of other people is about release of the illusion of control and moving on.

Can you find empathy in these everyday situations and understand these people have traveled their own private journey that manifested into what you see?

> » The micromanaging boss.

» The jealous significant other.

» The rebellious teenager.

» The overprotective parent.

» The paranoid client.

» The angry sibling.

» The attention-seeking child.

We often fail to accept others because of their behavior. We feel slighted, annoyed, upset and like they're treating us that way because of *us*—when they're not. They're treating us that way because of *them*, their journey, their values, and their worldview. By accepting them, exercising empathy for how they're showing up and whatever the underlying cause may be, you automatically treat the other person better and with greater kindness. You don't compromise your commitment to be your highest and best self. When you empathize, you break the cycle of hurt people hurting people.

By accepting others as they are, we can return our focus to ourselves, our own habits, and life journey. We can avoid getting caught up in controlling behaviors, anxiety, codependency, and self-destructive behaviors, all of which hurt *us*. Instead, we can focus on building lives that offer the most meaning and joy.

When you need some tools to work with for moments of struggle, try these:

» Ask what someone is going through and seek to get into their world

» Remove yourself from the equation and understand the person would be acting this way to anyone in your position (no matter what you said, or what you did—even for just breathing)

» Lovingly detach from the person out of love for yourself and them

» Look at yourself through their eyes, and ask if you're proud of who you're being in response

» Imagine they've been through something, and remind yourself that you don't need to know what it is to offer compassion and love

» Deeply listen with compassion if they choose to share

» Reflect on how you might think, feel, or act in that situation if the tables were turned

» Respond with love and kindness, and know in your heart *it's not about you*

A wallet-sized version of this list of tools is available at thesixhabits.com/resources. Print it out, keep it handy. While you're taking a deep breath in a challenging moment, refer to the list to respond with empathy.

REDIRECTION

We've already talked about the important skill of redirection, how it works, and how it applies to kindness.

Let's apply the same three-step process to acceptance, but with new examples, so you can see it in action and in a new light. Always keep in mind that although the 1-2-3 Knockout tool is the same, kindness and acceptance are different habits.

Before we dive in, I want to invite you to download the workbook I created to help you with this section, and you can download it at thesixhabits.com/resources. You may wish to print that out and have it handy *before* you go further.

Remember:

> » *Destructive:* thought, word, or action that destroys.

> » *Instructive*: thought, word, or action that teaches, informs, and advocates.

> » *Constructive:* thought, word, or action that builds.

Let's dive right into the process and see it in action.

DESTRUCTIVE → INSTRUCTIVE → CONSTRUCTIVE

Like with kindness, let's start with the simple destructive thoughts we have and build on them.

> » Destructive: I'm ashamed I've accomplished so little in my life.

> » Destructive: I will never forgive that jerk for what he did to me.

> » Destructive: I hate that I'm always so awkward

around people.

» Destructive: I hate how my friend is so needy and clingy right now. I can't get her to stop crying.

» Destructive: I wish I was smarter, taller, thinner, prettier, or pick-your-own.

» Destructive: I can't go to the beach in this bathing suit. Everyone will see how fat I am.

STOPPING THE DESTRUCTION

Remember, just like with kindness, to stop the destruction in acceptance, you have to catch yourself and then decide it's unacceptable.

GIVING OURSELVES INSTRUCTION

When you give yourself instruction, you need to focus on why you want to redirect, and what you get out of it. Remember, you are your own coach and your own advocate! Follow the thought process, using the same statements above, but adding in the instruction and supporting thoughts.

» Destructive: I'm ashamed I've accomplished so little in my life.

» Instructive: By focusing on what I haven't done, I'm completely ignoring everything I *have* done, and that's not going to help me accomplish anything else.

» Destructive: I will never forgive that jerk for what he did to me.

» Instructive: I can accept what happened, and I can forgive because it's good for *me*.

» Destructive: I hate that I'm always so awkward around people.

» Instructive: Affirming something perpetuates it, so I choose to affirm something good.

» Destructive: I hate how my friend is so needy and clingy right now. I can't get her to stop crying.

» Instructive: I want to be a good friend, but I can't be everything my friend needs. I am going to give her what support I can and remember my friend is going through a divorce and is dealing with a whole lot of emotions she wasn't prepared for. This isn't her fault, and she isn't herself right now.

» Destructive: I wish I was smarter, taller, thinner, prettier, pick-your-own.

» Instructive: I'm learning to accept myself exactly the way I am and wishing to be someone else isn't going to help me do that.

» Destructive: I can't go to the beach in this bathing suit. Everyone will see how fat I am.

» Instructive: Life is for living and hiding in my house is robbing *me* of joy. I'm not the only person that's overweight, and I don't deserve less fun than anyone else. I am worthy of having a great life regardless of my size.

Again, you need to use everything you know about why your destructive thoughts, words, or actions are bad, how they're hurting you, what you stand to gain by changing, and ultimately, your "why" to help you reframe. Your instructive comments to yourself can be just a few words, or they can be a full speech. It's fully up to you. Some of us respond best to something short and to the point. Some of us respond best to careful explanations. As long as you're providing yourself with the coaching and loving advocacy that you need, you're doing it right. Allow yourself to provide exactly what you need to get the best result.

STARTING THE CONSTRUCTION

As with kindness, generally, the easiest most obvious way is to start with the exact opposite of the destruction:

» Destructive: I'm *ashamed* I've accomplished so little in my life.

» Instructive: By focusing on what I haven't done, I'm completely ignoring everything I *have* done, and that's not going to help me accomplish anything else.

» Constructive: I am *proud* of what I've accomplished in my life, and I'm ready to do more.

» Destructive: I will never forgive that jerk for what he did to me.

» Instructive: I can accept what happened, and I can forgive because it's good for *me*.

» Constructive: I forgive him.

If that feels awkward or ill-fitting, restate that you're becoming, working on, learning to, growing in, getting better at, and so on:

» Destructive: I *hate* that I'm always so awkward around people.

» Instructive: Affirming something perpetuates it, so I choose to affirm something good.

» Constructive: I'm *learning* to become more comfortable around people.

» Destructive: I hate how my friend is so needy and clingy right now. I can't get her to stop crying.

» Instructive: I want to be a good friend, but I can't be everything my friend needs. I am going to give her what support I can and remember my friend is going through a divorce and is dealing with a whole lot of emotions she wasn't prepared for. This isn't her fault, and she isn't herself right now.

» Constructive: I am learning to accept my limitations and getting better at understanding that fixing her problems is not my responsibility.

If that doesn't quite fit either, use "I am" language to give proper framing to new thoughts, words, or actions that you're either working on or considering cultivating.

» Destructive: I *wish* I was smarter, taller, thinner, prettier, pick-your-own.

» Instructive: I'm learning to accept myself exactly the way I am and wishing to be someone else isn't going to help me do that.

» Constructive: *I am* smart, tall, pretty, pick-your-own, and *I'm* great exactly the way *I am*.

» Destructive: I can't go to the beach in this bathing suit. Everyone will see how fat I am.

» Instructive: Life is for living and hiding in my house is robbing *me* of joy. I'm not the only person that's overweight, and I don't

deserve less fun than anyone else. I am
worthy of having a great life regardless of my
size.

» Constructive: I am going to the beach, and
the only person's opinion of me that matters is
mine!

Whatever redirection language you give yourself,
make sure it's affirming the good and helping to reinforce
construction. If you take nothing else from both sections on
redirection, remember three important words:

» Destruction

» Instruction

» Construction

If you haven't downloaded the free workbook to help you
become a ninja at redirecting your thoughts and words with
acceptance, now's the time. Visit thesixhabits.com/resources.

THE BOTTOM LINE

Accepting yourself may be one of your life's greatest
challenges, but when you do, your ability to be happy becomes
second nature. Accepting others is the key to more satisfying
and rewarding relationships with those around you and with
yourself. Seek to empathize with others, even when you don't
know what they've been through or what's causing them to
show up the way they are. Redirect your thoughts when
you're struggling to accept yourself and others by noting the

destruction, giving yourself instruction, and then powerfully constructing new thoughts that serve you.

3. Gratitude

—————————— ∞ ——————————

Gratitude is the habit governing appreciation for all of life, not just the highlights. It is the embracing of the whole of a situation, finding the positive and the benefit in every aspect of life, even in something outwardly negative.

Gratitude is one of my favorite habits because it is one of the easiest ones to incorporate into your daily life, and the most immediately satisfying. After reading countless personal development books, spending time working with my coaches, meeting someone that genuinely inspired me, and helping someone I loved, I decided I needed to incorporate some gratitude back into my life. I knew I would be a happier person if I just got back to humble appreciation. Bear with me, I'm going to start with the results, then I'll get to how you can live your best (grateful) life.

Perhaps my favorite hashtag of all time is *#firstworldproblems*. Not only does it make me laugh, but it points out the absurdity of the majority of the things we complain about. We really do have it pretty darned good. I think about my own life. I am incredibly blessed, and yet I whine about silly little things just like everyone else does because things aren't exactly perfect in every single moment. I have bad days like everyone else. At this point in history, people in America and so many other nations are more spoiled than ever, and we certainly act like it—myself included. I point no fingers, I simply state what is.

Before we go any further, I want to preface this next part by stating upfront that it's going to sound quite a bit like I'm bragging, when in fact, I'm being profoundly and proudly grateful. You need to know the difference because very soon, you're going to start living the gratitude lifestyle right alongside me. Now, let's call out the stigma. Bragging isn't socially acceptable in our culture, especially if the one bragging happens to be a woman. I defiantly reject this idea and I love to see men and *especially* women brag largely *because* the stigma around bragging keeps us living in pain, which is what you and I are currently working to undo through this book. I know what my crazy gratitude looks like, and I'm not sorry.

I'm calling it out ahead of time so you and I can break the barriers that are holding you back from real joy and profound meaning in your life. If you're not proud of your gratitude, you're feeling shame. That shame is going to firmly hold you back. I want you to let it go and stop agreeing with the social norm that condemns happy people who are proud and grateful. I want you to learn to be so crazy grateful about your own life that you are an appreciation ultra-warrior and can feel as awesome about your own life as I do about mine.

What am I grateful for? I'm thrilled to tell you and here are some highlights. I'm thirty-eight years old, I'm healthy, I'm a size six, I'm reasonably attractive, I'm married to a man who would move heaven and earth just to put a smile on my face, and I own a company I retired from. I continue to get paid well and no longer have to work for it. I have an excellent relationship with my parents. I have a handful of amazing friends who love me for who I truly am. I sold my home that was nearly paid off and now live in an island paradise with comfort and ease, and so on. I've got it pretty good!

But wait, there's more! Let's go deeper. I overcame domestic abuse and went on to feel good about myself. I can forgive with ease. I put myself in a position where I could create my own life and create jobs for others. Even though I was tortured and made fun of as a kid, I was able to rise above it and become a good, kind, giving person. Even though I grew up on food stamps and my parents have always struggled because of my father's disability, I never went without, and now I have the opportunity in my life to give to the people who gave so much to me. And so on. Yes, indeedy, I do have it good!

Oh, but wait, there's still more. Did you really think I was done? No way! Let's go simpler. I woke up on this side of the dirt today. I'm healthy and clean air abundantly fills my lungs automatically and whenever I want it to. When I wake up in the morning, I have the luxury of choosing what I eat for breakfast and my arms move so I can feed myself. I can drive to the gym and pick things up and put them down until I want to pass out. I don't have to be afraid for my safety when I leave my house. I'm alive! My GOD, do I have it good!

Sounds a little like bragging, huh? I warned you! Here's the real picture. I have a beautiful life because I choose to see it that way. The previous statements aren't a laundry list of things that are right about my life. I am incredibly, ridiculously, obnoxiously grateful for every single gift I have been given, including the ones people routinely take for granted, and *especially* the ones that are more elusive.

You have an equally beautiful life with your own unique list of amazing things, and I want to help you see that beauty on a regular basis. I want you to be filled with the same incredible awe that will change your life. You might have less or more money than me, you might have less or more family than me, you might have less or more physical abilities than me. It doesn't matter. Whatever you have, those are your gifts. And as we all learned from the time we were little, it's plain rude not to appreciate the gifts you have been given. I want to teach you how to do it all over again and give you the gift of gratitude.

Let's dive in, go beyond reading, and apply this knowledge. There's a gratitude workbook waiting for you on thesixhabits.com/resources that you can use to help master this habit. As I talk about elsewhere in this book, you have to practice the habits you want to keep. They are all habits you need to develop, and like any other muscle, you need to routinely work at them so they get in good shape. Gratitude is a daily practice.

You might be considering your own life right now, perhaps reflecting on how your life is a disaster, and my life sounds better by comparison. Maybe that's true, maybe it's not. We'll never know either way. But what we do know is this—every life has beauty and blessings in it, even in the most remote and poor places in the world. You just need to look. If you focus on the negative, you manifest more of it, your mood suffers, and you can't get out of your own way. Doors are closed, you feel horrible on a regular basis, and you basically hate yourself. You don't need to have tons of money in the bank to be grateful and appreciative for the beauty of life. You don't need to look like the cover models on glossy magazines to feel grateful for the strong and powerful healthy body you were given.

One day several years ago, I noticed that for the millionth time, I felt extra lousy about myself, the world, and everything in it. I was busy mired in self-pity, feeling bad, feeling lower than low, and having absolutely no appreciation for the gifts in my life. My life had its difficulties to be sure, but that's all I could see. Because that was all I saw, I was remarkably unhappy. Maybe you can relate.

Then one of my dearest friends introduced me to her childhood friend. The man was in his early thirties and lived with his parents. He was one of the most incessantly cheerful, helpful, and uplifting people I have ever met in my life. He inspired me from the moment I met him. I loved his smile, his laugh, and the way he chose to share his joy freely. When he died about six years later, no one was surprised. We all knew it would come, and the world is a darker place without him. What made him so special? This man was in a car accident at sixteen years old that permanently rendered him incapable of caring for himself and doing the simplest things on his own, including breathing. This remarkable human being was bound to a wheelchair and while just a teenager, was imprisoned in his newly quadriplegic body for the rest of his life. And yet, *he chose to be grateful.* So many people would look at him and probably be confused about why or how a man in such an unfortunate situation *could* ever and *would* ever choose happiness. One of his greatest tools? Gratitude.

When he died, there was no funeral. Instead, there was a vibrant celebration of life. How appropriate for such a marvelous human being. One thing that stuck out to me and that I still remember with great respect is how he came to view his early moments on the ventilator as one of his life's greatest gifts. At the celebration, my friend shared a powerful story he had told her before he passed away. When he was first learning to breathe all over again and speak with assistance, he could barely talk, and it required great effort. This man was forced to choose his words carefully because every six seconds, the ventilator he was on helped his body take another breath, and he was forced into silence. The silence gave him a chance to collect his thoughts, choose his words carefully, and make the most of his brief windows of opportunity to speak. This specific gift, which probably felt like a curse in some moments, gave him the chance to become a person of intention. Many people just say whatever they want, me being one of them. Now imagine for a moment every single statement you want to make being interrupted like clockwork every six seconds with silence. How would you choose to respond? Would you respond with gratitude the way this man did? Or would you be angry and scream at God in frustration?

People tend to find gratitude as an act of desperation, not as a first step on their journey. I assure you that there were many dark days for this young man, and probably a few angry conversations with God. Still, he went on to inspire countless people and I am one of them.

When you take a look at your own life, are you truly and deeply grateful? Are you grateful for the injustices you've experienced? Are you grateful for the pain you have endured? Are you grateful for the unfortunate situations you've been through that have helped you become a better person? Are you grateful for life's gifts that you take for granted, like walking? Are you grateful for your life's gifts that you forget to be grateful for, such as your spouse who always leaves the toilet seat up? And are you grateful that you get the absolute privilege and joy of being *you*?

It's easy to get caught up in the day-to-day fray and insanity of our lives, forgetting to stop to smell the roses. But it's important to make the time. I need you to remember to say thank you for your gifts. This isn't so God or whomever or whatever you believe can bask in adulation, although that's nice. It's for *you*. It's so you are a happier, more complete, more fulfilled person.

There are 1,440 minutes in every single day. What could ever be so bad in only one, or even ten of them that would be worth ruining the other 1,430 for? Very little. Most of our lives are pretty mundane if you think about it, and that's wonderful. Of course, we all occasionally deal with death, tragedy, and so much more. Even through those moments, you can still practice gratitude and you will always find your way back to peace.

I have found that my greatest moments of incredible

clarity occurred when I was helping someone else. I don't think I really understood how gratitude could make an impact in my life until my husband, Amedeo, desperately needed my support.

Amedeo's grandmother, Nonna Maria, lived in a little town in Italy, and we lived outside of Boston. We had just booked flights to visit her. He was so proud to introduce me to Nonna Maria, and I was just as excited to meet her. For years, Amedeo's life was crowded with work and only had limited bursts of free time, so he wasn't able to make the long journey to visit her again until after we got married. His life and career changed when we met, and we were about to be on our way. He was overjoyed when he told Nonna Maria he was finally getting to go see her after sixteen years, and so was she.

About two weeks later, Amedeo received an emotional phone call from his cousin in Italy informing him that Nonna Maria had passed away. I've never seen a grown man cry so hard. Of course, he was sad, but more than that, he was overcome with regret and the pain of narrowly missing his last chance to see her ever again. He was devastated and was in a hole so deep I didn't think I could help him climb out. We talked and talked, and while it helped a little, the pain was unyielding.

I was desperate to do anything to make him feel better. Seeing the one you love suffer is horrible, and we all would do anything to take the pain away. We sat together, and I challenged him in a moment of clarity on my part (and rock-bottom sadness on his part) to write a list of fifty things he was grateful for in his life, including details about his life in Italy with Nonna Maria. He accepted. It took him a while, but he did it. At the end of the fifty things, some fifteen minutes later, his mood had visibly lifted. While he wrote the list, his facial expression softened. When he was done, his shoulders straightened, the sadness lessened, and the burden of the situation (while still present), was much easier to deal with—he was even smiling.

Those fifteen minutes went by quickly for him and slowly for me. I was practically chewing my fingers off in anticipation, hoping and praying that my little gratitude exercise would help him. I was anxious to see what would happen and discuss it with him after. Those fifteen minutes changed my life forever, and with the perspective and influence of my dear friend's inspirational friend, I was able to truly understand the absolute incredible magic and power of gratitude. I fully understood its impact on someone's quality of life and their ability to lead an amazing life regardless of their circumstances.

Immediately following that experience and seeing how much it helped Amedeo, I had the idea that I wanted to write out *my* gratitude every day and make it a part of my life permanently. I asked my husband to join me in this exercise every single night. He and I would grab a piece of paper, spend a few minutes, and write out the twenty-five things we were most grateful for that day. We would often read our lists to each other. We even put them on giant sticky notes and stuck them to the wall. We had quite the mosaic after a while. The results of my idea began to manifest themselves immediately and beautifully. Both of us immediately began sleeping better. Amedeo began quantum leaping through the healing process. We developed a deeper appreciation for and understanding of one another, and the things that truly mattered to us. It was a remarkable period of clarity that positively and permanently affected our lives. It continues to be our "go-to" method of cheering each other up and gaining immediate perspective amidst a bad situation.

FINDING GRATITUDE

What you and I are going to do together is learn how to search for the good and build the new habit of finding gratitude in every situation. As my mother would say, "Turn the shirt inside out." Sometimes you merely need to look at something differently and change your perspective to see what's truly going on. Anyone can choose to have a lousy attitude, just as anyone can simply choose to have a great attitude.

THE BASICS

First, let's talk about how to find gratitude. Sometimes when you're lower than low, you can't see anything worth saying "thank you" for. Sometimes the best place to start is by looking at your own body. Can you be grateful for the body you've been given? Can you be grateful for your freedom to move around in the world? Can you be grateful for the ability to fill your lungs with beautiful fresh, clean air? Can you be grateful that you have a strong body? Can you be grateful that you're alive and woke up today?

While the body and mobility subjects are basics because these are the gifts that allow us to have everything else, they are the things most often overlooked. Instead of complaining about the astigmatism in your eyes and how blurry the stars are, can you be grateful you can see the stars at all? Instead of complaining your back is hurting, can you be grateful your back has worked hard to hold you upright all these years and is trying to tell you something? Instead of noticing the extra weight around your midsection, can you be grateful for a body that keeps functioning for you and does what it knows to keep you nourished?

Can you be grateful you're reading these words right now? Start with the basics of what's right in front of you: *you*. Start there and I challenge you to create a list of twenty-five things you're grateful for, solely about your body, to prove to yourself this is easy. You can do it.

THE ADVERSITY

Once you go through the basics and feel thoroughly satisfied with yourself, it's time to move on to adversity and turning something unpleasant around. I make no assertions that this is easy. What vividly painful situations (or aspects of those situations) in your life can you look back on and be grateful for because of what they ultimately taught you or gave you? What situations can you feel genuinely grateful for because they shaped you into the amazing human being you are? What hurtful people can you be grateful for because they taught you lessons you didn't want to learn but that served you quite well anyway?

When digging through the wreckage of the past, we have to reexamine old wounds, and old feelings can bubble up all over again. This is painful, but an opportunity for *massive* healing. When you change your relationship with what happened and how you look back on it, you change the marks it leaves on you. I spoke plainly earlier about the abuse I endured and how I was grateful for what happened because it brought out parts of me I didn't know were there. The abuse and the overcoming of the situation taught me a lot about what I'm capable of. Moreover, it taught me the purest and most transcendent meaning of forgiveness. Take a look at your own life, and I challenge you to create a list of ten things you're grateful for, solely based on your painful moments. Look hard at each situation and ask yourself:

>> What did I get out of this?

>> What did I learn from this?

>> How did this ultimately change my life in a positive way?

>> Why am I a better person for having gone through this?

>> How did this experience shape others' lives in a positive way?

By taking a good hard look at a negative situation and

finding all the treasure it contains, you learn how to not only be grateful but also to leave the past where it belongs. You learn how to heal the wound that may have been causing you pain for years. Again, when you change your relationship with what happened and how you look back on it, you change the marks it leaves on you. What was once pain can become a beautiful mosaic of life lessons you appreciate.

THE LAYUPS

Once you've moved on from adversity, you can look at the fun gifts in life, the ones that are pure joy and absolute bonus material. Maybe you have an amazing spouse who adores you and thinks the world of you. Even though they do stupid things that annoy you sometimes (don't we all?), can you be grateful for their presence in your life? Maybe you've had a cat for fifteen years like I did. He was old, he pooped on the floor, and he cost me thousands in veterinary bills. But I still had my little friend by my side, unconditionally loving me through every moment, good and bad. Do you have something or someone like that you can be grateful for?

Can you be grateful for the children that consistently bug you for ice cream and never want to go to bed? Can you remember how badly you wanted them, and what life was like when you couldn't get pregnant? Can you find the gratitude in the job that drives you crazy and the long hours you have to work, knowing that it takes you away from your family sometimes? Is there any joy to be found in holding a position of such great importance that the company can't run without you? Is there any pride to be found in your family that is more comfortable and secure because of your hard work? Dig deep and look.

I challenge you to make a list of fifty (yes fifty!) great things that have happened or are happening *today*. If Amedeo can list fifty in one of his life's most difficult moments, so can you. Look at the questions I already posed, then try these to find the day-to-day goodies if you're not at fifty yet:

- » Why was my morning so great?

- » Why was my day at work amazing (even if it didn't feel like it)?

- » What wins from today can I celebrate?

- » Who told me they loved me today?

- » What am I learning that's getting me excited?

- » Who do I have in my life that I'd be lost without?

- » Who do I know I can always count on?

- » What am I looking forward to tonight?

Start here. Do fifty. This is such a powerful warm-up exercise for what's to come. Between The Basics, The Adversity, and The Layups, you will have a spectacular, mind-blowing, healing, feel-good list of eighty-five things to hold dear before you jump into what's next—which is super easy by comparison.

GRATITUDE IN ACTION

You can find gratitude anywhere you look, but you have to train yourself to look for it. So, here is the exercise we're going to do together on an ongoing basis. I needed to train you by getting the hard stuff out of the way first. Often when you go to the gym, you'll lift weights, and you're going to start lighter and work your way up to heavier. We're doing the exact opposite here. Training your brain can be different, and in this case, it is. Once you've developed proficiency in finding the gratitude, you won't have to do the heavy lifting anymore.

At the end of every single day, I challenge you to create a list of twenty-five thoughts of gratitude, specifically before you fall asleep at night. You can dictate them into a list on your phone and email it to yourself, you can write them in a notebook, or speak them out loud. Heck, text them to a friend and have a gratitude face-off! No matter how you do it, keep count. The actual quantity matters.

I would strongly suggest you do something in writing so you can look back at it later. Why? I'm going to specifically challenge you to never say the same things twice. At the end of thirty days, you should have a staggering list of things you're grateful for, starting with the eighty-five we kicked off with. Not only will this little journal be a reminder you can refer back to in moments of feeling lousy down the road, but it will also serve as tremendous inspiration for you and others in your life should you choose to share it. It will prove to you and others that the list is long, and you can indeed *dig deep*. I assure you, I could go on and on about what I'm grateful for in my life. Of all of the exercises in this book, this one will push you the most, force you to think the most, and will give you most incredible results the fastest.

You might choose to list twenty-five thoughts of gratitude every day for the rest of your life if you like. Please do!

THE BOTTOM LINE

Gratitude is a daily exercise for your brain—which needs a regular workout. With consistent practice, you will develop a strong muscle to help you identify opportunities for gratitude in your life.

Write twenty-five things you're grateful for every night before bed to change your life.

4. Presence

Presence is the habit governing awareness of what's right in front of us, staying true to the current moment, current needs, and current circumstances. It's the habit of learning from the past, looking forward to the future, but fixating on neither. Instead, it focuses on this moment, now.

It's hard to be present. Getting stuck in the past is easy and dreaming of (or dreading) the future is effortless.

We automatically remember and spend time reflecting on the bad day we had yesterday, the problems that happened to us when we were younger, the failed relationships we had, maybe a parent that abused us, how much we hate our job, etc. Just as easily, we can get lost in the memories of "the good old days" when we were younger, thinner, healthier, more successful, had the best job of our life, loved the president in office, and the kids were little, etc. The past is a blessing and a curse, and it is one hundred percent a valuable part of your life. I know how easy it is to get stuck there because I do it too.

Then there's the future—we *all* tend to think about tomorrow. The upcoming surgery we're dreading, the awkward conversation we need to have at work, a loved one's death, the birthday party we just don't want to go to, the painful conversation with our child about something they lost, etc. And then, of course, we think about the good things: what goals we're working on, what's on the agenda, who we want to be someday, the job, house, car, spouse, or vacation we truly want, and so on.

How could anyone be surprised that we all struggle to enjoy right here and right now? As a society, we're even trained to focus on yesterday and tomorrow, so it's not your fault for doing it. Here's how you can know it's not your fault:

> » The news talks about what happened in the past, and what will happen in the future.

> » Your job expects you to adhere to a schedule with timelines, dates, goals, etc.

> » Your family wants to know what time you'll be home.

> » You have to plan if you're going to go on a vacation.

> » You have to dig deep and outline your past if you want to get a great job in your future.

The challenge around presence is *time*.

When I was a little girl, there were two specific moments where I was fully present, and they continue to linger in my mind after all these years. Because nothing in particular was noteworthy or special, I was able to witness the magic of the ordinary and find beauty in something so plain. It was deep immersion *in the moment* that made the difference.

In the first memory, I was sitting quietly in the grass in my front yard during summer break. I was minding my own business and picking through the grass leisurely. I poked around looking for tiny little flowers, bugs, interesting rocks, extra-long blades of grass, all while enjoying how the wind felt on my skin. The sun was warm on my back, the wind rustled softly through the leaves in the trees, and the birds sang various songs around me. It was what I thought was the perfect temperature, and it was a beautiful day. It was not a particularly grand moment, but it was for me *because* it was so ordinary. I was fully present. I wasn't worried about how I had ended up in trouble the day before, or that I had to go back to school soon. Just for that moment, I was in heaven, fully aware of the here and now, enjoying the fullness of the moment and all it had to offer. It was so awesome that thirty-plus years later, I still remember it with perfect clarity. If I close my eyes and sit on the grass in the sun somewhere, I leap back to that moment as if I were experiencing it again for the first time. That's how vivid it was, and that's how delightful presence can truly be.

In the second memory, when I was a little older, I went down to the pond behind our house and sat by the little waterfall. It was nothing jaw-dropping crowds would "ooh" and "ahh" over, but my dad built up the area to add to a natural stream already there. To me, it was liquid joy. The waterfall descended two whole feet, burbled over rocks, and splashed into the purest small pool. It made a clear, reliable, white noise sound I always liked. I sat there while mosquitos munched my skin. I stared into the shallow pond of clear water searching for teeny little fish, baby bullfrogs, and more—all while appreciating the wonderful gurgle and white noise of the waterfall. I only heard the water, the birds, and the trees. I couldn't see my house anymore. I was alone in the woods, in my favorite spot, deeply enamored with how beautiful nature could be when we stopped to appreciate it.

As babies, we don't understand time. That's both a blessing and a curse. When we first enter the world, we are fully present, all the time. The joy of this is the fun, the lightheartedness, the innocence, and the pure thrill of discovering everything life has to offer.

As children, we begin to learn about time and its relationship to everyday life in society, while we still know how to appreciate the here and now. As we learn, we have to reconcile new knowledge (and societal expectation) against our natural-born desires to play, have fun, and be present with joy. As tiny-adults-in-training, we often get the nuances of societal life wrong and end up in trouble for falling behind, prioritizing fun, and avoiding the drudgery of responsibility.

As adults, we've absorbed enough repetition from the world around us to really get the hang of this time thing. We become great at scheduling, being punctual (well, some of us), managing the past and future, plus making it all somehow work. However, we get so good at it that we lose our natural-born ability to be present. We forget the gift we were given when we came into this world.

I'm not teaching you to be present. I'm reminding you what you once knew but forgot. Together, we are bringing you *back* to the state of joy and feeling truly alive by being present.

Getting stuck in yesterday and tomorrow is a terrible habit we acquire as we enter adulthood. We need to pay attention to our agendas, what's coming up on the calendar, and be mindful of the lessons we learned before. That's what adulthood is and what makes us functional members of a (mostly) peaceful society. What's not productive is focusing on those things to the point where we lose sight of the here and now.

I'll share one more memory with you, but this time, a not-so-magical one from my childhood—one that left quite an impression on me as well. My father was (and still is) disabled. He has a rare nerve disease that leaves him in a great deal of pain every moment of his life. He was injured when I was a year old and had surgery that didn't work out well. The medical procedure jump-started a pain disease called arachnoiditis, and though he can still walk and get around, he's been in extraordinary pain for as long as I can remember.

When I was a little girl, I wanted to do fun things with my dad. Sometimes he said yes, but for the most part, he said no because he was in too much pain, in a lousy mood, or not up for doing fun things. As a tiny human, new to the world and still fully capable of being present, I was confused. I took his rejection personally sometimes, and I didn't understand why he wouldn't just do the thing I wanted him to do *despite the pain*. My pint-sized logic was: "You're going to be in pain regardless, why not have fun anyway?" My dad didn't agree. For years it was like this, and he opted out of a lot. It affected me (and my mother), of course, but it affected him the most.

Skip ahead to today, and Dad doesn't opt out anymore.

He lives his life despite the pain. While it took him some years to figure it out, he decided missing out was no longer an option and that he deserved to have a good life. *He chose to be present.* He doesn't miss out anymore, he does fun things, and most importantly—he doesn't focus on what his body *can't* do. Now he goes on trips with my mom, they smile and laugh all the time, they have fun together, and he's genuinely a happier person. Sure, he's in pain (probably a great deal more than when I was a kid), his body is slowing down from age, but his attitude and focus on being present has changed his life for the better. My dad is living the best life he's able to and enjoying it. I couldn't be happier to see it.

My dad's journey has left an indelible impression on me. What he went through and all those years of missing out is something I've always been determined *not* to mimic. I deeply hope his story can inspire you to make the same determination for yourself.

Now, all that in mind, I've grown up, and I'm just as guilty as you are when it comes to living in the past or the future. I let my excitement for tomorrow make today look bad and I let my worry about tomorrow rob me of today's joy. I let yesterday's frustrations bleed into today and I let the victories of yesterday make me lazy today. While I have improved substantially since discovering The Six Habits and putting them into this book for you, I still have to work on this constantly. It's easier since I retired and moved to Maui, but I want to admit to you that I still struggle and have to put in conscious effort daily.

That being said, we are going to change this together.

What we're not going to do is beat ourselves up for what we've already done, or habits we've had for years. That's not going to serve any good purpose and would fly in the face of everything we talked about with the kindness habit. Instead, we're going to focus on what we can do right now (yes, now!) to build a new habit that will become as automatic as breathing someday soon, and we'll be happier for it.

I've done a lot of work on myself to where I am much *more* mindful and present than I was, and I used the presence exercises to do it. I'm getting better and better all the time, but for me, it's the toughest habit to master. This exercise is for you and me alike. We're going to practice being present together. Let's explore some examples that you might relate to.

BEING PRESENT AT HOME

Let's say you're a fairly new parent. You've got two little kids, filled with more energy than you ever thought was possible for a tiny human to have. Surprise! You're not getting enough sleep, you're not paying enough attention to your spouse, you hate your job, and you're tired. Basically, you're just an unhappy lump of skin and bones at this point. You're stuck in survival mode. Where is the joy?

What can you do? You take moments in your life and create purposeful presence. Let's say the kids are playing on the floor, raising hell as they usually do, and they want to play with you. You're exhausted, you're not in the best mood, and you have no interest. I appreciate not wanting to do something and not being in the mood. However, in this moment you can remind yourself how much you love those kids. How much they mean to you, and how fleeting this part of their lives actually is. You'll only get this day with them once, you only get this moment with them once, and you only get their childhood with them—you guessed it—once.

When you remind yourself of these things, you decide to play a game with the kids. You set your phone down, shut off the TV, and decide to be fully engaged. You stop focusing on your aching back, you stop thinking about how tired you are and how you only got three hours of sleep last night, how you had a crappy day at work, or how your spouse is giving you the stink eye because you still haven't done the dishes. You choose to be present with your children for ten little minutes. Maybe you even set the timer to remind you that you don't get to run off and be an adult again until the timer goes off.

What you give to your children and yourself in those ten little minutes is the gift of joy! You get to witness their excitement and how much they love *you*, love *life*, and are excited to play.

You laugh, you smile, you remember how to play, and get out of your head. You forget about work, bills, the dishes, and the boss at work. You too get to feel the bliss of living in the moment and share in the joy. Maybe you even lose track of time or shut the timer off and keep playing. Thanks to this moment with your kids and your decision to be present, you remind yourself that life is great, worth living, and loads of fun if you allow it to be. Children (and animals) are perhaps some of the greatest role models we have when it comes to learning how to be truly present.

Do you see redirection at work here? This (like many of the other habit skills in the book we talk about) is a muscle that requires regular exercise to become strong and healthy. After ten minutes of playing with your children and being fully present, *you are free, just like your children.* If you did it right, at the end of ten little minutes, your children's enthusiasm should infect you with the positive energy you sincerely needed. Take the win and do it again at your earliest opportunity.

BEING PRESENT AT WORK

Let's say you hate your job. You have a boss that's an impolite, unpleasant, micromanaging jerk. It seems like they only want to cut you down to size every opportunity they get, remind you of everything you're not doing, and never want to pat you on the back when you do a good job. You used to like your job once upon a time, but you resent it now. When you crush your monthly tasks, you never feel great about them anymore because it all feels hollow and pointless. Now, you want out.

In this kind of circumstance, it's difficult to be present and focus on the beauty of what's going on in the exact moment, much less see any at all. Naturally, you tend to focus on all the injustices that lousy boss of yours served up. It's easy to fantasize about the new job that you want and working for someone else. It's easy to envision the greener grass on the other side of the fence. It's difficult to appreciate the here and now, because the here and now isn't so great.

Believe it or not, you *can* find presence and happiness here. You decide to focus on the good, and search for it. You decide to focus your energy on the task at hand and find some aspect of your work you enjoy. In this example, the job itself isn't the problem—the boss is. You decide to hunker down at your laptop and focus on something you're great at and love doing. Before you know it, the hours whiz by, and you forget to even look at your phone. You're left with a rewarding feeling of personal satisfaction for your accomplishment, the pleasure you felt from doing something you sincerely love, and a big chunk out of your to-do list that's no longer staring you down.

In the moments when you don't have to deal with the boss, you can choose to be fully present, and focus on the aspects of your job you're good at, you take pride in, you enjoy, and you can be proud of yourself for accomplishing. You can do a great job *for yourself.*

When you selfishly decide to do a great job because you *want* to, not because you *have* to, you win. You get the privilege of feeling fantastic and choose to remind yourself that it's not the job, it's the boss. You received several hours in the zone without the boss, being fully present with what you love. You won because you separated the two ideas in your mind. The dark cloud dissipates, you feel renewed, and capable. That positive feeling leads to you having a better commute home, a better feeling toward life in general, a better conversation with your family when you arrive home, and better feelings of purpose.

By choosing to be present and doing a great job for *yourself*, you make your own life better and stop the suffering. The more you adopt an attitude of presence in your everyday work life, the more your attitude toward your job changes and you stop seeing it through such negative eyes. It's even possible that your boss notices the change in you because your attitude and productivity have made such an improvement. Your entire relationship with your boss might take a positive turn and you may even find yourself back to loving your job after all. At the end of the day, your choice to become present (one moment at a time) holds the potential to turn your whole situation around—if you let it.

Do you see redirection at work here too? After giving yourself a powerful redirection and shifting your attention to being present regarding what you *do* like about your job, you can and will feel better. You'll look forward to the satisfaction of a job well done, knowing you crushed it. You don't need validation from the jerk boss. You can feel confident about yourself and your job because you choose to.

WORK-LIFE BALANCE

Maybe you have this nasty little habit of thinking about being home when you're at work and thinking about being at work when you're at home. In that situation, you're essentially spending your whole life wishing you aren't where you are, and you're not appreciating that part of your life for what it is. That's not serving you at all.

In this moment, you can choose to be present with each situation by creating firm boundaries in your mind. Most importantly, in each situation, you must catch yourself and gently redirect. Let's explore the redirection in action:

While at work:

> » Destructive: I don't want to be at work right now—I'd rather be home.

> » Instructive: Focusing on where I am will help me to do a better job, derive greater personal satisfaction, and will help me be present when I *do* get home.

> » Constructive: I choose to be present at work, doing my best, and giving this my full attention.

While at home:

> » Destructive: I can't believe what happened at work today—I can't stop thinking about it.

> » Instructive: Focusing on work when I should be with my family robs me of my joy, my family's joy, and everyone suffers. With a rested mind, I'll be better for my family, and better at work.

> » Constructive: I'm grateful to be at home and I deserve to enjoy it. I am present.

When you successfully redirect yourself to be present

in either situation, reminding yourself of your reasons and benefits for doing so, you effectively force your attention to where it will be the most productive. You stop complaining, focus on the good, and allow yourself to be present—which in turn allows you to bring your best self to the situation. Everyone benefits: you, your employer, your coworkers, your clients, your spouse, your family, your children, and more.

When you're successfully present at work, you *will* do a better job, and you'll find you are able to advance your career much better. You will discover the ability to mentally punch out at the end of the day, which in turn gives you a better relationship with yourself and those you share your life with. You'll be a happier person. When you're successfully present at home, you are a better partner, better family member, and you find yourself in the proper frame of mind to approach work and life with gusto.

PUT YOUR PHONE DOWN

As a grown woman with a career, I often have my phone surgically attached to me. (Relatable, much?) This is a nasty habit I am working to break. My parents are in their seventies, and my father is disabled. They won't live forever, and I know it. Talk about not being present—I've spent my whole life worrying about the day they'd die and leave me. I shudder to think about it.

Though I have a half-brother who is fifteen years older, I was raised as an only child, and for seventeen years, it was just me and them. Through all the disagreements, Dad's disability, Mom's menopause, growing up on food stamps, getting my own hormones, and eventually becoming an adult, we love each other now more than ever. They mean the world to me and I cherish my time with them. Yet... I can't put my phone down until I remind myself. *I will not beat myself up.*

When I do remember to be present, I use the exact redirection technique I shared with you before:

> » Destructive: What's happening on Facebook is so interesting.

> » Instructive: Facebook will always be there, but this moment with your parents won't be. Put your phone down and enjoy their company.

> » Constructive: I choose to be present. There is nothing on Facebook that's more important than my time with them.

> » Destructive: I really need to answer my emails *right now*.

> » Instructive: I'm not a doctor, I'm not saving lives, and my parents won't always be here.

> » Constructive: I choose to be present. If something is *that* important, I'll get a phone call.

> » Destructive: I'm bored, this conversation isn't

interesting. What's on Instagram?

» Instructive: The conversation probably isn't interesting because I'm half-involved in it, and not paying attention. I can change the conversation to something great by being present and participating fully.

» Constructive: I choose to be present. This conversation is a two-way street and I choose to do my part.

» Destructive: I can listen and play with my phone, no sweat.

» Instructive: Multitasking is sucking at multiple things. By giving my parents my full attention, I get to enjoy their company and we all have a better experience.

» Constructive: I choose to be present. What phone?

More often than not lately, I've been able to focus and be fully present with them. I've been able to remind myself more to put the phone down, deal with whatever I need to deal with beforehand and actually show up for them, and for me. It's working, but like everything else, it's a work in progress.

When I am present and put my phone down, I've noticed a *lot* of benefits. Our conversations are better. I'm able to help them do things around the house. I learn interesting things about them and their lives before I was born. I learn their innermost thoughts as thinking and feeling adults (not just my parents). I have more laughs. I learn that I have more in common with them than I thought. I get great advice. I share what's honestly on my mind. I see the world through their eyes, and I reliably rediscover time flies by. I'm *always* left wanting more.

Of course, it's not all about me. They benefit tremendously too. They get to spend time with their daughter without having to compete for her attention. They feel heard. They get to know me and who I am as a grown adult (not just their daughter). They enjoy laughs with me. They do nice things for me. They get to make me smile and feel appreciated. They get to share their thoughts and feelings with someone who truly loves them. They get a friend that always thinks of their feelings and needs. They get an advocate, and they feel the respect they deserve.

Put your phone down! Are you guilty of doing this with your parents? Your friends? Your kids? Your spouse?

When you can successfully put your phone down, you are undeniably happier. You learn new things and ask better questions. You're able to give and receive all of the love and attention available. Your loved ones enjoy being around you more, and you enjoy being around them too. How can you use redirection to be present?

WHAT'S POSSIBLE AFTER YOU DEVELOP THE HABIT

Let me tell you about one of my recent opportunities to be present. I drove an hour from my house to have a meeting with someone at a restaurant. She had a new phone, and our appointment didn't show up on her calendar. I sat there by myself waiting, an hour from my house, and wasted over two hours of my day. However, instead of getting upset with her or the situation, I chose to empathize and enjoy how my plans changed—much to my surprise. I chose to enjoy walking around the lifestyle center where the restaurant was and checking out the stores. I chose to make a few phone calls and get a few things done on my phone, relishing the unexpected change of plans.

Once you get in the habit of choosing how you feel about something, incorporating a lot of the skills we talked about here (kindness, acceptance, gratitude, redirection), and choosing to be present, being a happy camper in *any* situation becomes a reflex. It won't even occur to you to get bent out of shape. I have a pretty well-developed muscle at this point. I could have been ticked off I didn't get to go to the gym because this appointment directly conflicted with the class I like to take. I could have been annoyed that I wasted two and a half hours of my day when I had a huge to-do list. I could have been upset she didn't call me before I left my house. Frankly, I could have been upset about all of it, but what would have been the point? It would have taken my happiness away. I chose to be present with a new moment I hadn't planned for. As a result, I was in a great mood, and when my lunch date called to apologize profusely, I accepted her apology with a laugh, holding no hard feelings. She felt terrible and even thanked me for responding so well to the mistake. She appreciated how good-natured I was being. Cool!

MINI MOMENTS

Choosing to be present is not automatic for us grown-ups anymore, remember? It's second nature for kids and even though we forget how to do it, I want to reinforce that our ability is still there. We just have to dust it off and remember how. Here are some mini moments where you can opt in to the present.

» Driving in the car in a snowstorm and choosing to enjoy the journey, how empty the roads are, and the pretty snow, instead of freaking out and being ticked off at how slow you have to go.

» Running late for something and letting go of the worry about how someone else might react when you get there—choosing instead to focus on arriving in one piece.

» Being at work and choosing to enjoy the task you're working on. Letting go of how you feel about being there just for now.

» When your flight is delayed, and you're stuck in the airport for four more hours. Choosing to use the four hours to enjoy your time in the airport checking out new things and perhaps making a new friend.

» When you first wake up in the morning and the house is still quiet, you have the whole house to yourself, and get to make coffee for yourself in silence. You choose to enjoy the feeling of the cold tile in the kitchen on your bare feet and the sound of the scoop digging into the coffee grounds, instead of focusing on how tired you are and the unpleasant schedule you have ahead of you.

» You're driving to get somewhere, and it's taking forever. Your butt hurts, and you just want the trip to be over. You could choose to complain about it and make the journey miserable, but instead, you decide to appreciate all the sights around you, and maybe play a game with yourself to enjoy the experience—since you're going to have the experience anyway.

» You miss your ex, you're lonely, and wish you had someone. Instead of being sad, you choose to focus on self-care, enjoying some activities you can't generally do with someone else.

» You're sitting in NYC traffic, feel your blood boiling and instead choose to call up Julie Andrews' version of "I Feel Pretty" (like Anger Management) on Spotify, blast it full volume, learn the words in seven plays on repeat, and sing out the windows to befuddled New Yorkers at the top of your lungs. (Wait, too specific? *wink*)

Can you think of any other examples where you can find the opportunities to be present? It's not always in the face of something going wrong. Sometimes it's about being present when things are going right or, as the way this chapter started, when things are perfectly ordinary.

Being present is not difficult to re-learn or remember to do. You just need to practice, and that's what we're going to do together. I challenge you to make one mindful choice every single day. Enjoy and cherish a chunk of time—which doesn't need to last longer than ten minutes. It can be any moment you choose—even your shower.

Savor the moment. When your day is over, specifically take time to recall what happened and write down all your wins with being present. Next, intentionally build your presence plan for the next day. I recommend journaling to keep you focused. You can download the workbook at thesixhabits. com/resources. Go back, reflect on a great choice you made, why you did it, how you did it, and how it felt. If you were able to do it more than once, journal about that too. If you're able to get so many points of presence in your day that you can start listing them off as you do with gratitude, wonderful! I fully support you.

THE BOTTOM LINE

When you focus on the past or the future, you're missing out on the beauty in right now (and there's a lot to be found *everywhere*). This is a habit we learn as we grow older, when once upon a time it was automatic. By being present, you'll find happiness, and you'll have more peace and appreciation in your heart.

Practice redirection to help you to catch yourself when

you're not being present, identify your need to be present at every possible opportunity, and show up. Be sure to find your compelling reason for being present. Choose to be present forcefully, and actively push aside all other thoughts or tasks for a small period of time (set a timer if necessary). Allow yourself to experience the here and now. There is beauty in the mundane if you choose to see it.

5. Goodness

—————————— ∞ ——————————

Goodness is the habit governing energy and what we allow, invite, and build into our lives. It is the habit of actively removing toxic and harmful (though often gratifying) energy from our lives, and actively adding positive, beneficial energy into our lives.

NEWS & SOCIAL MEDIA
—————————— ⟪⟫ ——————————

The world is a mostly good place. If you watch the news or pay attention to too much social media, you might vehemently disagree with me. The news and social media are both filled with negativity, hateful people being angry or fighting with each other, and heinous acts that make you sad to the core. The late comedian Bill Hicks once famously said, "We're a virus with shoes." If you're constantly absorbing continuous streams of negativity about the world and the people in it, how could you possibly see it any other way?

As a person who has had quite enough of being made to feel bad, I opted out of television news years ago. I don't even have cable (on purpose!). When I was a kid, the news was always on. I remember thinking how depressing it was, how the newscasters were always so morose, and how it became part of my "normal," even though I hated when it was on. One time, my aunt came to visit, and I asked her about the news and what she liked to watch. I'll never forget her reply—it made so much sense. She said, "I don't watch the news. It's all bad news and I don't want to know." Unsurprisingly, my aunt is one of the happiest people I know.

The fact is, good news doesn't sell. I spent twenty years dealing with the media, and not much has changed. Television, newspapers, magazines, and radio broadcasts are forms of media that exist predominantly on advertiser and subscription revenue. The reason why news outlets focus so much on the negative is because it gains more traction, gets higher engagement, gets more clicks, and spreads on its own.

Countless psychological and scientific studies have been done proving people prefer negative information to positive. In order to compete with the TV shows, sitcoms, game shows, reality shows, articles, kitten pictures and more, the news outlets need to give people what they want. To do that, news is often blended with entertainment by reporting on news stories in ways that are highly dramatized, and objectivity is removed in favor of opinion and speculative journalism. It's all delivered to you in small bites that you can consume in mass-quantity without reprieve. This method helps media and news outlets sell more corporate sponsoring and advertising spots because they have more viewers who stay engaged longer. This method also helps to sell more subscriptions because the drama creates a sense of "need" for the "infotainment" presented.

Think about it, the news is *not* actually the product being sold—*you are*—and it's costing you your mental health. Graham Davey, Professor Emeritus of Psychology at Sussex University and Editor-in-Chief of the Journal of Experimental Psychology, is quoted as saying, "The way that news is presented and the way that we access news has changed significantly over the last fifteen to twenty years. These changes have often been detrimental to general mental health." Many people are becoming rich at the expense of your wellbeing. Are you okay with that?

Social media isn't much different than the mainstream media anymore, and the two have begun to merge in recent years. Your home page on Facebook is the "news feed" and there are top headlines within a scroll or a glance. Your feed on Twitter is one big venting session mixed with news and promotions. Added to that are your friends who stoke the fire by talking about the news, unwittingly sharing fake news, opining on the news in general, venting about it, adding more bias, and introducing community outrage.

Let's not forget about all of the other ways social media is negative. For starters, it's a black hole where hours can be lost in the blink of an eye. It can suck us into comparison because what we see can make us feel bad about ourselves. It's also addictive and tricks us into thinking it will make us feel better when it actually makes us feel worse. Finally, it has been proven to socially isolate people and make them feel lonelier and more separated from others.

The madness needs to stop. Let's rip off the bandage. It might hurt, but it'll be less painful if we just get it over with. I challenge you to eliminate or drastically limit your exposure to this onslaught of negativity for ninety days. You'll be able to notice the difference after a few days to a few weeks. Your mood and your heart will be lighter, plus you won't feel so hopeless about humanity (or your role in it).

I'm going to challenge you to do two things. Depending on who you are, this might be easy or hard for you. Challenge Number One: eliminate or drastically limit news from your life for ninety days. I urge you to watch different things on TV or shut the television off entirely and be with your family or friends. Read a book instead. Opt out of biographical accounts of horrible things throughout history in the way of books, magazines, or articles. Don't pick up the newspaper for your own sanity. Challenge Number Two: eliminate or drastically limit social media for ninety days.

I imagine you probably think I'm crazy and you're already saying in your mind, "Nope, I'm not doing that." I completely understand, believe it or not, and even as I write these words to you, I feel a bit of hesitation myself. I'm thinking of how much I like scrolling through Facebook, but then I have to be honest with myself and admit I don't like it as much as I think I do. I have never enjoyed watching the news, so that is not going to be a difficult thing for me to opt out of.

Once upon a time, I found so much value in Facebook, and for my career, I still do. However, I don't like seeing humanity at its worst. I hate seeing people fighting and insulting each other in the comments section, being "keyboard warriors," and trolls. It's horrible. If you've never taken a look at the comments section before, take a quick look at a few things you find interesting and potentially divisive, then see how terrible people are to one another. It's disheartening.

After ninety days, you can expect to find yourself

thoroughly detoxed and ready to ditch social platforms for good or dramatically reduce their role in your life. Give it a chance and accept my challenge.

Are you worried you won't stay informed? Don't. If something *that* important happened, people in your life will tell you. As I'm writing this, I'm remembering Burt Reynolds died yesterday. I don't watch the news, and I didn't see it on social media. I was spending time with my parents, celebrating my dad's birthday. My mom told me. And now I know—without consuming any news. If other people choose to watch the news (and they will), that's their prerogative. This book is about you.

Social media and the news are both addictions. You convince yourself you need them, but you know deep down that you don't. They are habits like anything else. You just need to get out of the habit of consuming them, and once you do, you'll realize how far down the rabbit hole you were. Once upon a time, you were able to live your life without these things. Do you remember being a kid, blissfully unaware of how horrible the world seemed, and not even knowing what social media was? I remember those days and I was a heck of a lot happier then. I want that back—for both of us.

There's really something to the saying, "ignorance is bliss." In doing my research for this book, debating if I wanted to pepper it with quotes (I decided against it), I learned the true quote is actually: "Ignorance is bliss, 'tis folly to be wise," and it's attributed to Thomas Gray, an English poet. Thanks to my research, now I appreciate it even more. The more "informed" I was in my life, the less happy I felt. The more

I focused on my own little corner of the world, myself, and what good I could contribute, the happier I became. This still holds true.

Still not convinced? There is no safe way I've found to consume the news, and if you're wholeheartedly going to commit to the process, I challenge you to give yourself ninety days, cold turkey, without the news. When it comes to social media, you might not need to be so severe.

While I would strongly suggest you opt out of social media entirely, another alternative would be to create a new profile and start over. It's going to be a lot easier than scrubbing and cleaning, and it might be more satisfying than completely opting out. Depending on who you are, you might find it more satisfying to completely say goodbye to it for three months.

If you decide to hang onto social media, I suggest doing one or more of the following:

1. Go through everything you have ever liked, and **scrub all of the content**. Unfollow any account that is controversial, political, or makes you feel bad. Unfollow anything that shows humanity at its worst in the comment section. Unfollow people who are negative, make you compare yourself to them, or generally make you feel bad about yourself.

2. **Create an entirely new profile**. Start over. Add the friends you love the most and can't live without. The people you know are never negative—the people you spend time

with, in real life. *Focus on quality rather than quantity.*

- With Instagram, I already did this, and I'm very intentional about the accounts I follow. I went on a "following spree" one day and followed accounts related to travel, food, art, creativity, positive quotes, health and wellness, kitties, puppies, scientific facts, and everything else I find to be genuinely interesting. These accounts don't put trash in my mind. As a result, I enjoy Instagram and it *never* makes me feel bad. I've made it safe.

3. **Use the "lists" feature on Facebook** so you can keep your existing account without much work. In my case, I set my homepage on Facebook to be a list that I've created of nineteen people I hang out with, people I am related to, the person I am married to, and the people who always make me happy. The list is short, and instead of going to the homepage on Facebook, I now go to the newsfeed (via the button in my bookmarks bar) for only that list. It is so much easier.

   - Given that Facebook and all other forms of social media seem to change weekly, I'm not going to outline instructions for you to do the same thing here, but I would encourage you to do a quick Google search, ask someone, or just click a hundred buttons until you figure it out.

4. **Limit your time.** I have been known to waste a few hours by mindlessly scrolling. You too? I suggest you create a time limit for yourself. Set a timer on your phone and give yourself a maximum of fifteen minutes on social media. If you don't think you spend too much time scrolling through social media, get a stopwatch going at the beginning of a browsing session and just let yourself have a good time. Spend as much time as you like. When you're done, I think you might find yourself astonished at how much time you spend there.

Focusing on goodness and seeking to create a greater stream of positivity by creating space for it allows you to put yourself in a better headspace. A better headspace allows you to feel better about yourself. Feeling better about yourself allows you to pursue the things you most want, make the changes in your life that would most inspire you, and genuinely enjoy your one precious life.

TOXIC PEOPLE AND THINGS

When it comes to the subject of goodness, we can't fully explore the idea without talking about toxic *people*. Sometimes they're friends, and sometimes they might even be related to you. Toxic people, whoever they are, are a continual drain of energy, happiness, and your general will to live. You might not always be able to limit your exposure to these people, but you should try your best.

Some years ago, I had a friend who appeared completely

positive and awesome when I first met her. She and I would go out, we'd laugh, hang out at home, and be each other's confidante. We grew closer, and as trust grew, the relationship became more vulnerable. You know you've hit that special place in a new friendship when you can talk freely about what scares you and weighs on your mind.

This vulnerability was something I appreciated and valued. It was wonderful to be able to share openly and have the honor of someone trusting me in return. But, unfortunately, it was the very thing that led to the end of the friendship. As we became closer, a dependency emerged. My friend was going through some legitimately and understandably painful things that broke her heart, made her question herself, and she needed someone to talk to. I was happy to listen—that's what friends do. I listened, and listened, and listened some more. I became a lousy, unpaid therapist. I gave everything I had to give and then dug up more. I admit at the time, I didn't know how to create boundaries and felt incredibly inappropriate for even wanting to have any at all—after all, my friend was in pain.

What I couldn't see early on was my lack of boundaries and the dependence she had on me went outside the lines of a healthy friendship. One was giving constantly (me), and the other was taking constantly (her). This was taking a toll on me and our friendship. I've always led with my heart, and I worried about her all the time, feeling so helpless and in over my head. Her stress became my stress, and her pain became my pain. I was losing sleep because I felt so drained, negative, and stressed out. I even started to see my own world through a negative lens. The dependency continued to escalate into daily "counseling sessions," venting, and crying. My own negativity intensified as I became more depleted. Negativity was starting to take over my life, and I kept thinking that things would get better soon.

She began abusing her prescription medication and her behavior spiraled. One night she even went so far as to threaten suicide by overdose and stopped answering my texts and frantic phone calls. I was beside myself. Naturally, I dropped what I was doing and did what I could to intervene. I raced to her house in the middle of the night, hoping to save my friend. When I got there, she yelled at me for taking her seriously and "creating drama." I was confused, bitter, angry, and empty.

The friendship terminated not long after because I couldn't take the high cost of the relationship anymore. Before it ended, I communicated how I felt. I told her that while I cared about her deeply and wanted to fully support her on her journey, the way I'd been supportive up until then was taking a toll on me and it couldn't continue. My attempt to establish healthy boundaries was too late. The response was essentially, "You're being a bad friend." I tried to get her to see that I genuinely cared and wasn't abandoning her, but I just couldn't sacrifice my own well-being anymore.

With all of the sincerest love I had in me, I gently suggested she see a therapist to help her navigate her tough situation. It was fully warranted. She declined. I tried another angle and suggested she take some time for herself and practice some self-care—she again declined. I tried to preserve the friendship, empathizing with her pain, but feeling so depleted and like my own needs didn't matter to her, I was forced to reevaluate everything.

I could finally see that I had co-created an unhealthy relationship. I was as much responsible for it as she was. I had let my own desire to be needed and valued cloud my judgment and convince me boundaries were inappropriate. Despite that, I sincerely wanted to correct the situation and create a healthy friendship going forward, but as I said, it was too late. Ultimately, the friendship dissolved when I finally realized my well-being mattered, and I needed to advocate for my own happiness with the same intensity I'd advocated for hers.

In hindsight, it's hard for me to begrudge her for her behavior. We're just not rational when we're in that much pain. Not only that, if someone keeps showing up to help when we need it, it's easy to get dependent on the relief they provide. That's essentially what happened.

This is a great example of a toxic relationship because it started innocently as they always do. I chose to show up with love, ignoring my own needs, and the relationship became toxic to my well-being. I acknowledge my failure to establish boundaries earlier in the relationship. Perhaps the friendship could have continued if it had occurred to me sooner and I followed through. This is also a great example of a toxic relationship because my friend didn't mean to be toxic—she wasn't a malicious person. As we talked about earlier, hurt people, hurt people. She was hurt by others long before I met her. She couldn't see my needs as valid because of the enormity of her own needs, and the well-established pattern I was complicit in creating by never having any boundaries with her.

When people mistreat us in a toxic manner, it's ideal to forgive and empathize, but we mustn't sacrifice ourselves in the process. We deserve goodness in our lives and in our hearts. Sometimes, the only thing we *can* do is walk away. It hurts to leave, but it hurts more to stay.

I wish this was the only time in my life I had someone incredibly toxic around me, but that's not the case. I have toxic people around me now, and some of them I can't *eliminate* from my life. I do my best to avoid these people as much as I can, and my life is better for it.

Finally, there's the matter of toxic *things* that make you feel terrible. Maybe it's going to the all-you-can-eat buffet. It's fun for some, but maybe you hate yourself for three days after and it triggers eating disorders still in the back of your head. Perhaps it's the porn that feels so gratifying in the moment but ends up taking you away from real physical intimacy with your spouse. Maybe it's the cigarettes you can't put down after twenty years of trying. Maybe it's the alcoholism or gambling habit you've been denying you had for many years. Whatever your toxic issue is, get away from it the best you can.

If you struggle with addiction, this is an opportunity to look in the mirror, accept who you are, the choices you've made, and radically love yourself anyway. It will not be shame, but instead radical love that will help you finally take control of what happens next. Get professional help if you need it. There is zero shame in seeking support to conquer an addiction that's hurting you.

CREATING BOUNDARIES

Many people think creating boundaries is a bad thing and feel guilty for doing so. This is usually because the idea of boundaries is largely misunderstood to be something that separates us. In fact, boundaries are clear rules of engagement for healthy relationships. Here are some baseline facts about boundaries for us to build on:

» Boundaries are healthy and allow people to enjoy *better* relationships.

» Boundaries promote clear, honest, respectful communication.

» Boundaries help others to understand how you wish to be treated.

» Boundaries can be created respectfully and without discomfort.

» Boundaries are difficult for people who have unhealthy relationships with themselves.

» Boundaries are yours to create and are for others to respect.

» Boundaries not enforced will often be ignored.

While boundaries are the ground rules for a healthy

relationship, they can also highlight chaos in a toxic relationship, helping you see how things really are. Many of us love and work with people who are unhealthy, damaged, and haven't worked on themselves. This is where boundaries are even more important and start to get difficult.

Healthy relationships have lots of boundaries and we often don't realize it. We can comfortably communicate our needs and they're usually met, albeit with the occasional misstep, and the relationship is enjoyable overall.

By contrast, toxic relationships are relationships that are a lot of work and they cause pain to one or both parties. These relationships often leave us feeling exhausted or bitter. Think about a manipulative parent who uses guilt as a tool, a spouse who breaks promises and lies, or perhaps a boss or client who always criticizes and applies pressure for more than agreed. Toxic relationships are everywhere in varying degrees, and if we're experiencing one from the inside, we must take ownership of what *we're* doing to co-create it.

But wait! Hang on. Aren't we the victim when we're in a toxic relationship? Isn't the toxic person being abusive and hurting us? How are *we* co-creating anything? While *yes*, the abuser is hurting us, *we're complicit because we're choosing not to stop them, when we have the option to.* When we co-create a toxic relationship, we're not doing it intentionally. In fact, it's the lack of intention that's responsible here and contributing to the chaos. When we fail to create and enforce boundaries, we're inviting others to treat us however they feel. This can show up as nasty comments, greedy demands, passive-aggressive posts on social media, sustained physical abuse, excessive time demands, contract breaches, workplace exploitation, offensive conversations, inappropriate requests, and so much more.

I want to be very clear here and draw a line between toxic relationships and victimization. They are not the same things, and the difference is *control*. When someone is victimized, they have no choice in what someone else does to them, and any control over the outcome has been taken away from the victim by the abuser. Victimization is when someone is beaten, raped, stolen from, sabotaged, or any other awful thing where the victim truly has no control. By contrast, toxic relationships, which are what we're talking about here, can keep you under the *illusion* that you have no control, when in reality, you do. The difference between toxic relationships and victimization is *control* or the lack thereof.

That all being said, when we fail to master the habits of kindness and acceptance, it's easy to believe we have no control. However, *many of us would rather bear the discomfort of a toxic relationship than bear the discomfort of creating and enforcing boundaries.* This is a heartbreaking preference, not victimization.

Take a moment and visualize someone who you have a toxic relationship with. They could be a boss, client, a sibling, a lover, a parent, a child, or a friend. Hold that person's image in your mind, and let's look at the relationship. Ask yourself:

> » Do I dismiss small hurtful actions, refusing to classify them as abuse?

> » Do I make excuses for them when they hurt

me, saying things like, "They don't mean any harm," or "They didn't mean it"?

» Do I feel uncomfortable with the idea of pushing back against their behavior?

» Am I afraid of what they'll say or do to me if I confront them?

» Am I guilty of staying quiet to avoid conflict?

If you're answering "yes" to these questions, you're in a toxic relationship. It's time to learn about boundaries so you can either restructure the relationship and create new terms of engagement or decide to walk away.

The concept of creating healthy boundaries with others begins with belief in our own independent value and right to exercise free will. Social scientists call this "agency." I call this Habit Mastery, and it begins in kindness and acceptance. When we radically love ourselves and treat ourselves with radically loving behavior, we aren't willing to tolerate toxic behavior from *ourselves or others*.

If you're reading this book and haven't started doing any of the work or downloaded the workbooks, you may not have started to master kindness or acceptance yet. I urge you, *please* do this work on yourself. If you don't, creating boundaries will never feel good and it will always be awkward. I know you don't want to be in a toxic relationship. I also know you don't want to feel powerless. You can grab all my bonus material at thesixhabits.com/resources any time.

Over the years, I've been in all kinds of toxic relationships.

I've had clients who pressured me to do more work for the same amount of money. I've had friends take advantage of my generous nature. I've had family demand that I work for free then scold me when I decline. I've had people I care about freely insult me or talk down to me. I've had just about everyone ask to borrow money and unfailingly get upset with me when I say no. I've even had a lover lie to me about his sexual addiction, giving me a complex.

When people behave like this, we don't deserve it, nor do we need to tolerate it. Mastery of kindness and acceptance allows us to remember we don't deserve mistreatment and empowers us to act through goodness and create boundaries. Boundaries encourage healthy relationships to get even better and toxic relationships to reveal themselves.

You'll know you're in a toxic relationship when you create a boundary, it's not respected, and you confront the person. Their reaction tells you everything you need to know about any capability of having a healthy relationship with you, their ability to take responsibility for their actions, and their desire to respect you. Always remember people treat you the way they feel inside. If you're in a relationship with someone who doesn't have a respectful, loving relationship with *themselves*, how can you expect them to have one with you?

Creating boundaries starts by getting very clear with *ourselves* about our own terms. We often leave out this step and assume we all have the same values and standards, when we don't. Inevitably, when something negative happens within any relationship, someone gets upset because a boundary was crossed. The trouble is, the one with the boundary didn't specify it, and therefore, the one that crossed it doesn't know what they've done.

Avoid the drama and figure out what your boundaries are upfront. Communicate them early and often. Ask yourself what you feel your rights as a person are. Then, ask yourself what the limits of your physical, emotional, financial, spiritual, and sexual comfort are. Deeply explore your feelings and how different areas of life make you feel good, which areas make you feel bad, and why. Get clear.

Next, evaluate which relationships could use minor tweaking, and be prepared to discuss your clear boundaries. It's not easy, and if you're new to boundaries, I want you to start with the healthiest relationships you have. I want you to have early wins so you can see the benefit of boundaries and have the courage to dive into tougher conversations with more difficult relationships next.

To establish your boundaries, always be direct, concise, and respectful. State your needs clearly and offer the other person gratitude for listening, for caring about you, and for allowing you space to freely ask for what you need. Don't be vague to avoid discomfort.

For proactive conversations, write down your thoughts on paper if you're nervous and bring your notes with you for your own reference to keep you focused and brief. For conversations in the moment, focus on stating your needs in a positive, respectful, and objective manner. Do *not* turn the conversation into a huge emotional display—it doesn't need to be one. In creating a healthy relationship with others, we need to invite room between us to communicate freely about their needs as well as ours. Blame, judgment, and guilt have no place in a healthy conversation about boundaries. Keeping things positive and objective helps to invite easy communication and paves the way for even more. This is how incredible relationships are made.

To assert your boundaries within a toxic relationship, follow the same advice, but emotionally prepare yourself before you go into the situation if you can. It might get ugly. You can't control other people's reactions, and you want to be ready to remain positive, respectful, and objective *no matter what the other person does*. If you lose your cool, you're just as toxic. You must understand other people's journeys may cause them to react poorly to *any* boundaries with *anyone*. Don't forget that no matter how they react, *it does not negate your need for healthy boundaries*.

When we assert our boundaries and they're respected, we flourish and thrive within healthy, easy relationships that make us feel good. Toxic relationships *can* be turned around with clear feedback between both parties and a strong mutual commitment to create something better. Unfortunately, most toxic relationships need to be drastically reduced or fully eliminated. As someone that's done both, I can tell you that while it's stressful in the moment, when you're finally free, it's like the weight of an elephant has been taken off your chest and you're free to live your life in peace. It really is worth it.

TIME TO GET POSITIVE

First things first, you need to be mindful of your energy in the first place. Self-awareness is something you will learn to develop over time. Maybe you're incredibly self-aware already. If you are, congratulations—keep going! If you're not, this is a great time for you to learn how to be.

Self-awareness is knowing what you're doing, what you're saying, how you're showing up to others, your impact on others, your impact on yourself, how you feel, and why you feel it. When you're self-aware regarding your mental energy, you're in tune with whether your mental energy is positive, negative, or neutral. This awareness gives you more control over where you can steer yourself, which is self-regulation. In this chapter, we're trying to focus on steering away from the negative and steering toward the positive. Mindfulness, awareness of your energy level, and *quality* of energy will serve you well for the entirety of your life.

PEOPLE WHO ADD GOOD ENERGY

Surround yourself with good people who lift you up and make you feel good. These are not just people who are the opposite of toxic; they're more than that. These are people who are infectiously positive and rub their good energy off on you. These are people who make you laugh, who find the glass half full, who do fun and healthy things that you enjoy (like games, travel, outdoor activities, etc.), who don't make excuses, who enjoy living, and are grateful. When you can create a circle around you full of positivity and good energy, you're able to stand on the shoulders of giants.

They say you're known by the company you keep, and you are the average of the five people you spend the most time with. That is some *truth*, my friend. If you're constantly hanging around with people who are relentlessly negative and complaining, who can't get out of their own way, and who always find what's wrong with the world, how can you possibly bask in any goodness at all? You can't. You're not being exposed to it.

If you don't have an abundance of positive people in your life, you need to go out and find them. While many view making new friends as an adult to be hard, particularly for introverts, it's not *that* hard once you know what you're doing. You just need to know how, which is by putting yourself in circumstances where it's more likely. Having recently moved 5,000 miles away to an entirely new place where I don't know many people, I've been living this truth ever since. Here's what works:

> » Creating events that center around the kind of person you are and aspire to be, designed to attract like-minded people like you to attend. You can promote these on social media, or tools like Meetup or Eventbrite. You can also go old-fashioned and hang flyers if that works in your community.

> » Volunteering for organizations that share

values with you, specifically asking to be paired up with others in the work itself. You can find many great nonprofits and feel-good groups online or by calling local Chambers of Commerce.

» Joining business groups that cater to people in your shoes (such as entrepreneurs, stay at home moms with a side business, etc.).

» Joining social clubs with a mission you can support and that have regular meetings.

» Signing up for classes where there may be a social component, or at a minimum, you share interests with the other attendees. Yoga, meditation, art, cooking, gardening, etc. are all good ideas of classes. The more you go, the more people will see you, and connection will be easier.

» Searching online for events that are in line with your interests, causes, and beliefs. For example, you could find an awards night for a nonprofit you're considering supporting and attend that event.

Accompanying the things to do, these are the behaviors to adopt:

» Make it known you'd like to make new friends. No, you're not going to look like a loser. You're making it easier for *other* people to make friends by making your intentions clear. It's not easy for people to admit it, but if you take the lead, you'll be pleasantly surprised.

» Invite people who spark your interest to do something fun with you. Lunch, drinks, physical activities, etc. are all positive, friendly ways to start building relationships.

» Invite people again when they don't say yes immediately. People forget how to make friends as adults. Lead with love and let them see your invitation is the real deal.

» Ask about how to get involved and what kinds of social interaction are available where you could join in. Seek to learn and soak up all the info you can get.

» Let people know you're on the hunt for great organizations and events to attend where you can expand your social circle. Ask for referrals and links.

» Say yes to everything you're invited to (at least the first time). Try things at least once.

» Talk to people and learn about them.

» Add searching for events, classes, and organizations to your repeated tasks. As you find them, continue to go. Soon, you'll be in the enviable position of being able to hand-select your closest friends because they reflect the same values as you, and you can welcome them into your Inner Circle.

» Accept that rejection is part of the process, and

don't allow yourself to take it personally. You will invite people to do things, and they won't want to for their own reasons. You might hear excuses or flimsy reasons. You must expect it, plan for it, and follow the actions and behaviors *anyway*.

PEOPLE WHO ENCOURAGE YOU TO GROW

Do you hang around with people you admire? People who inspire you? Do you hang around with people who get you excited to do cool things? Or are you dragging people along for the ride? I love to be friends with people who inspire me, people who live their lives out loud, and people who take risks and do bold things. Just being around them challenges me to think bigger and push myself to grow. What kinds of people challenge *you* to think bigger and push yourself?

If you are inspired, that's all you need to know. You should want to be in the company of those who *propel you forward* and propel you toward everything you want to have, want to do, and want to *be*.

As I mentioned, at the beginning of 2018, I made a commitment to be kinder to myself and to launch a new business venture. I put myself out there for business conversations despite being the socially shy introvert I am, and I came across some pretty inspiring and courageous people along the way. I have developed fantastic new friendships that challenge me.

I wasn't looking for or expecting these friendships, but

they showed up anyway, and I am even more blessed. I took risks. I put myself out there. I (gasp) talked to people. I made actual friends. ME. Through these amazing new friendships, my comfort zone is continually challenged and I'm growing as a person. I found friendship, but also kinship and a source of unlimited inspiration.

If you don't have an abundance of inspiring people in your life, you need to go out and find them too. Follow the list of action items and behaviors under "Positive People." The process of adding more inspiring people in your life is identical.

THE GOODNESS LIFESTYLE

Read the following with the idea you're reading a menu, and you only need to pick out your favorites. This is your meal, your life, and your good things. Here are a lot of great ideas for things that will help you *add* positivity to your life. Choose one, choose five, but please don't choose all of them. That will create too much overwhelm and you won't do any. Set yourself up for success and choose at least one and no more than five (for now) that resonate with you. Figure out how to incorporate these good things into your life. You can always add more once you've developed a successful relationship with a few. The list is presented alphabetically without any other priority.

Affirmations

The power of affirmations is widely known in the personal development community. If you feel like you could use extra energy, give yourself extra affirmations. Use powerful statements to put yourself in the present moment of enjoying what you don't yet have. Use "I am," "I have," and "I love" language whenever possible.

Here's a made-up example. I want to open a plant shop, and I haven't done it yet. I'm nervous and have insecurities around whether or not I'll be successful. My affirmation for the plant shop might look like this: "I am *so* happy and grateful my plant shop is wildly successful. I get to make people smile every day!" I'll say this out loud and often. I'll say it as much as I need to until I believe it in my bones.

These are five rules I live by when creating my affirmations and self-talk in general:

1. When talking about something I want to do, I talk about it in the present tense and treat the idea like it's already happening.
   - Such as, "I eat healthy foods."

2. When talking about something bad for me, I reframe it to take the negative out.
   - Such as, "I am proud to be sober" instead of using words like "alcohol" or "drinking."

3. When talking about something I'm changing, I make sure I only use positive words.
   - Such as, "I floss every night" instead of using a statement like "I'm done going

to bed every night without flossing."
The "done" and "without" are negative
and should be avoided.

4. When adding in my feelings on the matter,
I talk about how I want to feel (much like
Instruction!).
   • Such as, "I love running every day
     because I feel healthy and filled with
     vitality."

5. When building something I'll stick with, I
keep it short.
   • Such as, "I affirm myself daily."

The magic in affirming lies in repetition. At first, you
might feel silly writing these down, or saying them out loud. I
suggest writing out five powerful affirmations daily (that can
change or stay the same day-to-day), then say them out loud
with conviction and power. If you feel like a nut for doing
this, go in the bathroom or do it in your car. The power is in
the vocalization and the delivery. If you say these affirming
statements with a whiny, bored tone, it's not going to affect
your life. You're wasting your time. If you say these affirming
statements with a powerful voice, authority, and confidence
(even if it's fake!), it *will* begin a positive chain reaction.

Art

Not everyone is creative, and many folks can't draw their
way out of a paper bag. If that's you, don't take off just yet—
this section has something for you too.

Create for the sake of creation, not the end result. For

those of us who can create beauty and magic on whatever canvas we choose, do it. It's therapeutic, relaxing, forces you to be fully present, and for some, it is a deeply spiritual experience. Create. Paint. Draw. Bake. Sew. Whatever it is that lights your soul up, do it.

For the people in the world that generally create for the sake of creation (like me), you already know creation is the classic double-edged sword. While it's cathartic and satisfying to create, it can also lead to feelings of never being good enough (ahem, Tortured Artist Syndrome). That in mind, I offer this particular piece of goodness with a warning: *create, but before you do, intentionally decide whatever you create will be good enough. Decide you will be purposefully present—and enjoy the process, irrespective of the final product.*

If you choose to direct your energies to getting better or gaining deeper proficiency, do so because you love what you're doing, *not* because you feel inadequate. Creation can be brief or span extraordinary lengths of time. Maintaining joyful presence will be a challenge if you don't powerfully choose it upfront and remind yourself along the way.

For those of us who can't create anything they're proud of from nothing, you can still enjoy the magic of art. The power of enjoying art is in letting go of any idea regarding the end result. It's not a test. No one is grading you. Bring yourself back to childhood and remember when you would draw and doodle because it was fun. Maybe you can go to the store and get an adult coloring book, a paint-by-numbers canvas, or even something aimed at kids. Better still—sign up for an adult art class. It's not silly, it's liberating. The point of art is the art itself, and the magic that is created during the process of creation.

Blogging

Journaling on paper or in digital form such as a blog, and exploring your thoughts, can be a great way to clear your mind. It can also clarify your thoughts and dreams. It's a great way to find others with shared thoughts and interests too. WordPress blogs are free. You can get a domain online, or you can use a free WordPress blog without one. I had a blog for a while and I really enjoyed it. My friends were the only readers, and they appreciated my insights. I got positive feedback about how my open thoughts were helpful to some of the things they were going through. Helping others while helping yourself is the very definition of a win-win.

If you find yourself loving the idea of blogging, you may decide to keep up with it and that's wonderful. Many people have blogs and will post every few months or so, many others post daily. Please regard this as something to add to your life for *you*–not revenue. If you create a blog as an outlet for your thoughts, it will be a wonderful contributor of goodness to your life. If you create a blog as a revenue stream and don't back it up with a business plan and a whole lot of work to support said business plan, you're just going to get frustrated. The idea of goodness will fly right out the window.

Be clear about your intentions for the blog right from the first word you type and give yourself the gift of expression from a place of purity. Blogging in this context is much like journaling, except you're sharing your thoughts with others who might see links or stumble across it.

Books & Audiobooks

I like driving. I like reading. It's hard to read *and* drive. It's bad for your health.

What's good for your health is listening to an audiobook while you drive, which is what I do. I wholeheartedly recommend listening to audiobooks while you clean the house, do the dishes, run errands, work out, drive, etc. At thesixhabits.com/resources, you can download a list of my favorite books. Give them a listen, or a read if you can carve out the sitting-still time. I don't make my recommendations lightly, and each one is one hundred percent worth it if you can invest the time and energy.

When I first listened to audiobooks, I would find myself annoyed I couldn't remember all the information contained and wanted to take notes. One thing I've found helpful is to find the chapter list in the audiobook software (I use Audible), then take notes on that after. You can also make a bookmark, take a screenshot and print it or save it to your phone. Chapter titles are often the only notes you need, as they are the principal take-away points from the book. If this isn't the case, you can often Google the book's summarized main points and find an image containing everything you need.

Clean Your House

I am fond of saying to anyone who will listen: "An organized mind is a productive mind." One of my favorite energy boosters is cleaning my house. I sincerely enjoy

178 I **The Six Habits**

cleaning my house because it allows me to clean my mind and organize my thoughts. I will often double my power and put an audiobook on my Bluetooth speaker while I clean. When I can look back around my house and see my home is in order, my mind is clean. I have a sense of accomplishment, and I can enjoy the results of my hard work.

This isn't to suggest you need to do a deep dive into every corner of your home and organize your shirts alphabetically according to brand (though if that's your thing, go for it). This is about putting things in their proper places, cleaning surfaces, removing clutter, folding the laundry *and* putting it away. This is about feeling a sense of completion, wholeness, and satisfaction.

Without fail, if I am feeling off-kilter in my work or projects, I clean my house and it gives me incredible clarity and *momentum* to keep going. The satisfaction of getting everything in order by itself is joyous and hugely motivating. However, the real power is in the fact that I've been in beast mode for an hour or more and achieving success against dust bunnies. A victory is a victory, and your brain doesn't know the difference.

Once your home is clean, you'd be surprised how fully capable, energized, and motivated you are to tackle the scary things on your to-do list.

Eating Right

I love healthy food. I also love unhealthy food. I don't think there's any shame in either. However, sometimes you feel shame when you choose something not great for you that makes you happy in the moment. What's wrong with being happy? (Here's a hint: nothing!)

For me, eating right means eating mostly healthy and having what I want the rest of the time, just *less* of it. Essentially, moderation. What "eating right" means for you might be something else. Whatever it looks like for you, it's worth a shot. Practice kindness when eating and try to let go of some of the unhealthy relationships with food (most of us have them) that keep you in a cycle of choosing poorly— which ends up making you feel bad.

In full transparency, I have had an unhealthy relationship with food. As a woman in America born in 1980, I have been bombarded with decades of messages implying I'll never be good enough unless I'm prettier, thinner, fitter, have bigger boobs, and a smaller, perfect butt with long, thick hair. On top of it, I've dealt with unspoken corporate expectations dictating I look a certain way and achieve at the same pace as my male counterparts. I have to do all of this while needing to be a beautiful woman (but not too beautiful), a sexy woman (but not too sexy), and a vocal woman (but not too vocal). These messages translated to an unhealthy relationship with my body image, and accordingly, an unhealthy relationship with one thing I felt I could control: food.

Here it is. I love food and eating makes me happy. *I don't eat to live; I live to eat.* Unfortunately, for years, I would deny myself the pleasure of enjoying food, believing that if I avoided it and opted for the "right" choice, I would finally fit the ideal I thought of what I was "supposed" to be. The problem is: it didn't work. I'd binge at night, depressed and needing to "cheat," so I never really enjoyed what I was having nor was I mindful. I *escaped* into food. I didn't know how to love food the way I do now, and it didn't love me back.

My weight fluctuated for years, and I'd lose twenty pounds and gain ten. I'd lose ten and gain thirty. And so on. I could never keep my weight steady and judged myself harshly no matter what I did. When I'd lose the weight, it was never enough, and I hated how I looked, even though I now realize I always looked great. When I gained the weight back, I also hated how I looked, even though I always looked great then, too. The messages made me feel insufficient no matter what I did or how I looked. I was miserable.

I got sick of feeling so much negativity around something I loved and wanted to have a joyful, mindful relationship with food. I decided I didn't care anymore about the messages and leaned into The Six Habits, starting most powerfully with kindness. I gave myself permission to enjoy the *very best* of what I wanted, whenever I wanted, without criticism or judgment. Instead of buying $2.00 low-quality ice cream at the grocery store because it's on sale, I now buy the best on the market and happily pay top dollar for it. Because the taste is *so* extraordinary, it is deeply satisfying. Because it is so satisfying, I was surprised to learn I don't need to have *as much* of it. I spend roughly the same as I was before. I'm satisfied with less in terms of quantity because I'm giving my soul, mind, and taste buds what they want: the very best experience.

The key for me has become *presence* with food, coupled with *kindness* toward myself when I do what makes my heart happy. The unexpected side effect was the automatic healing of my relationship with food. When I set out to find my happiness and discover The Six Habits, I *wasn't* expecting to heal my relationship with food. I'm pleased to share that I'm happier, and for the first time in my life, I'm at a weight that holds steady without thinking about it. I love how I look, I feel great, and I'm enjoying every single meal. I more frequently choose *better* foods because I want to, not out of begrudging obligation. I still enjoy ice cream and rich, fatty foods when I crave them. I finally learned how to love food and to receive that love back.

We all feel better about ourselves when we eat right, even if just for a day. If you're having a bad day, having a great, healthy relationship with food, *even just for the day* will boost you up because it's a win. You may not change your relationship with food (or need to) right away, but it's possible through the habits—most notably kindness, presence, and specifically, goodness.

Exercise

If you're like me, you probably don't love exercise, but once you get going, it's not half bad. Movement is mental lubricant. Using your body is a great way to stop using your head for a while. Taking fitness classes can be fun and can give your brain a break, one that you might sorely need. You might find working out on your own is more your speed. Or perhaps going for a hike and being with nature is what tickles you.

Whatever it is, find a way to move your body and take care

of your earthly vessel. Make a habit of incorporating little amounts of physical movement into your daily routine and start small if you're not super active already. Begin with the dedication to take a simple five-minute walk and *don't* break the promise to yourself. Schedule it into your day if you need to. Once you're feeling good with your regular walk, bump it to ten minutes. From there, you can keep inching it up, or you can substitute it with another form of movement.

As for me, I make it a point to have at least twenty minutes of phone-free movement every day. It typically ends up being more than that, but I promise myself the twenty minutes and keep it. I can't stand doing the same things all the time, so I switch it up. Now that I live next to the ocean, I often go for coastal walks. Sometimes I bring my dog, sometimes I bring my husband, and sometimes I go solo. I'll go for a hike with a business partner instead of sitting down to eat and talk. As I'm making new friends, I'll invite them to do something physical with me instead of sedentary (this is met with a *lot* of enthusiasm). I go in the forest, I swim in the ocean, I do laps in the pool, or just tread water for a while. Sometimes I'll take four little five-minute walks. Whatever it is, I move, and I take the stairs ninety percent of the time.

Your older self will thank you, your heart will thank you, and your mind will benefit. This could also be classified as "Treat Yo' Self" if done right. Start by asking yourself what sounds the most fun and how you could incorporate five little minutes of movement into your daily life.

A Full Night's Sleep

Easily, one of the most powerful things you can do to give yourself more positive energy is to get a full night of quality sleep. For a lot of people, this isn't possible, and I fully know that. If you can, and you have the luxury because you have the availability in your schedule, it's worth trying. Maybe clear your morning and catch up on some sleep. There's no shame in giving yourself restorative sleep, despite what the world might want you to think. Let go of any negative feelings you have around getting the sleep you need, such as calling yourself lazy, and be kind to yourself. If you need sleep, then sleep.

I feel obligated to call out the social media influencers and thought leaders who brag about their lack of sleep, then make their audiences feel the pressure to sleep less so they can achieve more. *It's the wrong message.* I fully and wholeheartedly disagree and refuse to support that idea. Furthermore, using a platform to spread a toxic message that is physically harmful both in the short and long term is irresponsible. Here's the actual truth: if you want to achieve or do more with your time, focus on your *efficiency*. However many hours you're awake, make the best of them and use them wisely. *It's not how many hours you have, it's what you do with them.* You can quote me on that.

Like I discussed with food, it's about *quality*. The same is true of waking hours in the day. The Mayo Clinic recommends adults get at least seven hours of sleep per night. Our bodies need adequate amounts of sleep to recharge the body from the day's activities. Proper sleep also restores the brain so we can feel rested the next day and perform better in our mental tasks. Sufficient sleep prepares us for what lies ahead— including a healthy life.

Don't believe the hype and just get your sleep. Listen to your body and when it's tired, punch out. I enthusiastically go to bed at 9:00 p.m. some nights. I don't stay up to watch TV, read books, or finish my task list. I just rest. I look forward to my rest. It makes all the difference for me, and it will for you.

Meditation

I adore meditation. As a strong Type A personality that's a go-getter and constantly busy, as well as a person with ADHD, the ability to quiet my mind has been a challenge most of my life. When I found meditation, I didn't think I could do it. I figured I was too mentally active to find stillness. I am so pleased to be wrong. Through meditation, I discovered a way for my mind to finally know what stillness is.

Many people think of meditation as that stock image that everyone is familiar with: a woman sitting on a mountaintop at dawn in the lotus position with this incredibly blissful look on her face and her back straight as an arrow. While that's lovely, and also entirely possible, that's not quite daily life. Meditation is much more accessible and easier than you might think. Sunrise mountaintop optional. If my hyperactive brain can do it, yours can too.

I have five favorite ways to meditate. I'm sure there are hundreds more, but these are the most powerful for my busy brain. Here they are:

1. **Breath Counting.** Get comfortable, even if it's lying down, and close your eyes. Try to breathe in gently to a slow count of four, and out gently to a slow count of four. Count your breath, but only on the exhale. Count to twenty-three exhales. Every time you lose count (and you will in the beginning), start over. When you get to twenty-three, start over at one. Set a timer for ten minutes, or however long you want. This gives your mind a toy to play with and makes it difficult to be distracted by your other thoughts or tasks. I have found it is remarkably effective for me when my brain will not shut up—which is basically all the time.

2. **Observational Listening Meditation.** Again, get comfortable, set a timer for however long, and simply observe. I close my eyes and listen carefully. I observe and I make *no* judgments. I listen to the sound of the cat walking across the floor, the sound of the clock ticking in the hallway, the sound of the refrigerator motor clicking on. I listen and observe life happening all around me as a detached and non-judgmental witness. If I hear my husband come in the door, I listen and observe his steps. If the cat is meowing at me, he can wait a few minutes. I observe and listen to his voice, without pressure to get up, pet him, or do something in response. The trick to this method is removing opinion and assessment of what you hear, not making mental notes about tasks you need to do, and not feeling moved to do something about what you hear. You are

the observer not doing anything other than witnessing life. It takes practice.

3. **Observational Walking Meditation.** This can be done when you are up and moving around. Your eyes should be open softly, with a gentle gaze and your energy focused on the ground in front of you. You slowly and purposefully walk in a circle for a period of time or you walk outside and get lost in the act of walking to free your mind. During your walk, you observe without judgment. This form of meditation, unlike the previous form, is a non-judgmental activity for the *eyes*. You observe the bug walking across your path, the multi-tonal details of the gray sidewalk, the snow crunching under your feet, the shoelace that's perhaps tied slightly askew. You do it all without judgment, or the need to fix or respond. Much like observational meditation, walking meditation takes practice.

4. **Intentional Wandering.** Perhaps my favorite meditation, intentional wandering is the most freeing type of meditation. You engage by getting comfortable, setting a timer, closing your eyes, and letting your mind wander. Your mind can be completely unencumbered or restricted. For some people, this isn't a good idea because the brain wants to go to all sorts of places, including problems, worries, to-do lists, etc. However, as you develop mastery of The Six Habits, it will become easier to get to the point where your mind doesn't go straight for the negative. Instead, you can let your

mind wander creatively and your job is only to be a casual observer of what your brain does when you're not controlling things. It can be truly magical. I've had some of my best ideas and most profound realizations through this approach.

5. **Kōan**. I like how Merriam-Webster defines a kōan: "A paradox to be meditated upon that is used to train Zen Buddhist monks to abandon ultimate dependence on reason and to force them into gaining sudden intuitive enlightenment." For me, the non-monk mortal, I love to get comfortable, close my eyes, and reflect upon a kōan because it's not about the answer, it's about the abandonment of reason and opening the mind to possibility. A widely known example is "When both hands are clapped a sound is produced; listen to the sound of one hand clapping." With this form of meditation, the statement, story, or question becomes a plaything. You're not expected to arrive at an answer, but instead to observe your mind and what it does as it ponders the kōan. You ultimately tap deeper into your own intuition and knowing. Can this be spiritual? Absolutely. Intellectual? Sure, but that's missing the point (remember, it's not meant to be solved). Confusing? Possibly. That's why I like it.

I enjoy a ten- to-fifteen-minute meditation, no matter what the method. Once I get into it and the timer goes off after ten or fifteen minutes, more often than not, I'm disappointed and want more. By then, the "spell" is broken, and I'm back to reality.

You might love all of these, or just one. I encourage you to not only try them all, but to try them all again and again at different stages in your Six Habits mastery journey and you'll note different experiences. Your favorite will emerge. If you love the idea of meditation and none of these seem quite right for you, start researching your own methods or go to a group meditation and talk with the leader about options that may suit how your mind works.

Podcasts

A podcast is a series of spoken audio episodes on a wide range of subjects. I have been a guest on several incredible podcasts and depending on when you read this, my own should be going strong with loads of engaging content to inspire and create possibility. Visit lauradibenedetto.com to listen. I like podcasts because they are highly digestible content, similar to an audiobook, but typically for free and shorter. They're generally anywhere from five minutes to sixty minutes, on a myriad of topics to include personal development, professional development, business matters, and a whole wide world of crazy ideas, novels, stories, etc. If you can think of it, there's a podcast for it.

You can find and browse through podcasts on iTunes, Spotify, and many other leading platforms. Listen to a few minutes of each and before long, you'll start to develop a collection of great podcasts to follow. Many of your favorite thought leaders will consistently invite you via their social media channels and emails to tune in and will give you instructions on exactly how to find their podcast.

Retreats

I am a huge fan of retreats, and there are many different kinds. There are silent retreats, retreats with active and thematic programming, and then those geared towards rest and relaxation. They range in price and levels of posh, and you can find them all over the world to suit nearly any budget or interest. Retreats can last one day or several weeks and can be held at a retreat center or hosted by your favorite thought leader. The world of retreats is expansive and continues to grow.

My favorites have featured several programs of varying lengths and intensity, including yoga, meditation, food relationships, diet, dance, music, play (yes, really!), sleep, and much more. A recent indulgence I enjoyed was an R&R retreat where you could opt in (or out of) anything. You could enjoy the beautiful grounds, savor the silence of the environment, and commune with others in a place of judgment-free quiet and bliss.

To find something that's up your alley, ask yourself the following questions, then get searching online:

1. Would I like to go to a retreat alone or with a loved one?

2. What's my budget for transportation, lodging, and programming combined?

3. What do I want to get out of the retreat?

4. What does my body most need right now?

5. What does my life most need right now?

6. What does my spirit most need right now?

7. What duration of time can I commit to this?

8. Where would my dream destination be?

9. Can I combine any travel dreams with my retreat intentions?

10. When is the ideal time for me to do this?

11. Of my favorite thought leaders, whose retreat(s) would I like to attend the most and why?

Now get searching! Don't be afraid to try something you can do for an afternoon nearby if your budget is restricted. I promise you, there is a retreat for everyone, and free afternoon retreats *do* exist.

Seminars, Workshops, & Conferences

These are amazing, fun, get you fired up, and expose you to like-minded people. They expand your worldview and let you immerse yourself in everything you're focusing on. The bigger the event, the longer the duration, the greater the high. Also, the bigger the crash when you return to reality. The beauty of these events is found *at* the event. It's up to you to take the magic home and *keep it going*. Many people forget that part.

My best advice when it comes to seminars, workshops, and conferences is to definitely *go* to some periodically, but don't aim to change your life the second you get home (you likely won't). Be very selective about which events will earn your time and money, and what *limited* pieces of advice you will deploy upon your return home. It's advisable to prioritize and enthusiastically accept only a small number of core ideas that suit you. Few people are capable of radical life transformation inside of a few days, and it's good to keep grounded so you can see results.

Make a point to seek out others while you're at whatever event you go to, and work to build relationships. You'll want to find like-minded people to keep in touch with. These relationships can help you sustain focus on priorities and help you maintain momentum.

Sharing the Sacred Vault

Being vulnerable can be hard. It's hard for me, and I'm a pretty open person. However, when I am vulnerable, I find that others want to lean in, be there, and show up with their best selves to be supportive and non-judgmental.

In the context of this book, I want to encourage you to be vulnerable with just a few worthy people. First, identify the ones who are worthy of your "deep, dark, and uglies." Ideally, you'll be asking for a Sacred Vault that holds secrets and vulnerabilities. It will be loaded with love and trust that goes both ways. This Sacred Vault is important for us to have throughout our lives when we're busy growing and reflecting. We need safe spaces for us to sort out and explore the messiness of our jumbled thoughts and feelings as we go about our lives, particularly when we're on any growth journey. The Sacred Vault allows us to be our true selves without judgment and to grow the way we most authentically desire.

Some of your Inner Circle relationships should have a Sacred Vault already, even if it hasn't been recognized as one yet. Identify who you share one with now, and specifically discuss it with the person. The act of identifying it clearly for both of you, as well as discussing its existence, will create a tighter force field of safety around what you already have. Tell your loved one what the Sacred Vault means to you and reaffirm the mutually agreed upon rules for the vault, *especially if they've only been assumed and not yet spoken about between you.* Tell them how you truly feel, what you're afraid of, what you're working on, who you want to be, what you dream of, and that you're reading The Six Habits. Perhaps you can even ask for open dialogue and accountability around your journey.

If you don't have any Sacred Vaults yet, you can create them within your Inner Circle with a little bravery. This is about increasing the intimacy within your Inner Circle and inviting your loved ones closer. Put yourself out there to one or a few people who you trust the most and ask to co-create a Sacred Vault with them. In your request, explain what a

Sacred Vault is, what it means to you, and what you propose the rules to be. When your loved one agrees to create a Sacred Vault with you, define and agree upon the rules before you share. Then dive in. Ask for open-minded love, safety, and freedom to be your fullest, most flawed self. Yes, actually ask. Be clear about what you need, and what you want in return. Once a Sacred Vault is created, you should first test the integrity of the Sacred Vault with something small, and see how that feels for both of you. Make sure that what goes in the Sacred Vault *stays* inside it. If it feels good and the person honors the Sacred Vault, keep going.

Does the idea of vulnerability scare you? Here are a few gentle conversation starters to try:

1. "I had an idea, and I want to run it by you. Since we trust each other already, I thought we could talk about creating a Sacred Vault. Essentially, it's an invisible lockbox for the things that are hard to talk about. We already share a lot, but this would be for the most vulnerable things. What do you think?"

2. "I need a safe place to share ideas and my innermost thoughts. Because I cherish our relationship so much, I wanted to approach you first. I'd love to explore the idea of creating a Sacred Vault for each other so we both have a safe place to share and be vulnerable. Can we have that conversation?"

3. "I love our relationship, and I love that I can

trust you. I'm wondering if we can create a Sacred Vault for the extra personal stuff so we can both share openly, without judgment. Any interest?"

Take a Class

You can always take a class on personal development, but I mean taking a class to learn how to do something you've always wanted to do. Maybe you'd like to learn about ballroom dancing, pottery, watercolor, mixed martial arts, Zen gardening, arc welding, speaking another language, guitar playing, sword-making, or the fine art of making French macarons. When you intentionally continue your life's learning in fun areas that expand your creativity, you get out of your head and become a happier human. Double points for bringing someone you love with you to experience it together!

How to get started? Check local newspapers, event websites, local high schools and universities for adult life classes, and *specialized* universities. Also check local organizations, museums, nonprofits, and clubs. I love to cook, so when I did my initial search, I found culinary classes at a specialized university an hour away from my home and ended up going to several. I had a wonderful time and I'll never forget it. I also did art classes at a nearby museum and learned some great new skills. Just look, ask questions, and be willing to try something new.

TED Talks

TED Talks (ted.com) offer an amazing and intellectual look at a myriad of ideas, spanning subjects like human sexuality, interpersonal relationships, curing cancer, designing roads in Nairobi, and solving global water crises. You name it, and it's there. TED stands for Technology, Entertainment, Design.

The TED stage brings forth some of the best ideas and presenters the world has to offer. I listen to TED Talks while doing other things and sometimes will pull them up on the TV to watch. Why do I recommend these? Learning is awesome, and these videos will leave you curious, full of wonder, full of appreciation, and feeling inspired. I've started many lively conversations with, "Hey! I just watched this amazing TED Talk and you're not going to believe this, but…"

I love TED Talks so much that I dreamed of giving one. Right before this book was published, I was invited to speak at TEDxMCPHS in Boston. I'd love for you to see my TED Talk and share the experience with me. Visit thesixhabits. com to check it out.

In addition to mine, I'm excited to share a few of my favorites that got me fired up, smiling, and ready to take on the world. Go look for:

> » Maysoon Zayid's talk entitled, "I got 99 Problems, Palsy is Just One"

> » Emilie Wapnick's talk entitled, "Why Some of Us Don't Have One True Calling"

> » Simon Sinek's talk entitled, "How Great

Leaders Inspire Great Action"

I appreciate how TED Talks make me *think*, and I know you will too. You can find TED online through their website, their YouTube channel, or their App. Explore, wander around, and click on talks you wouldn't normally click on. You will be pleasantly surprised to discover how many amazing ideas are out there just waiting for you.

Treat Yo' Self

I shouldn't need to say *much* here, but I do think this part is important. Self-care is important to your ability to function in your life and be at the top of your game in every role. Have the glass of wine, get the manicure, buy the movie, go to dinner, eat the cake. Just live your life and quit feeling guilty or bad about it. Life's too short.

Start by making a list of things that make you feel great and attach both a dollar figure and a time measurement next to it. Maybe the glass of wine is nine dollars and no extra time. Maybe the movie is fifteen dollars and two hours. I'm asking you to make the list because you're building a menu for yourself. I want you to stretch yourself as you're making the list and look for things that are easy, free, expensive, and complicated. Run the gamut and make the full spectrum list. How long should the list be? Go for fifty. Too easy? Go for one hundred. I'm dead serious. This is *your* menu to refer to when you get stuck. Make it awesome.

Keep the list handy and I challenge you to pick from the list at least four times a week, considering your time and budget when you choose. You deserve to Treat Yo' Self. I give you permission—can you *give yourself permission?*

Visualizing & Vision Boards

Visualization is the act of focusing intently on what you want to manifest in your life. Specifically, you envision (mentally, visually, or experientially) yourself already enjoying the successful manifestation of your goals.

Let's say you want a Mercedes Benz, and you can only afford a 1982 Yugo without a radio. You would visualize by either closing your eyes and picturing yourself behind the wheel of the Mercedes you want (mentally); by staring at a picture of the Mercedes you want every day as you brush your teeth (visually); or by going to a Mercedes dealership and taking one for a test drive (experientially). That's visualization. The objective is to get your brain to believe it already has the thing, idea, or life you want. You are fully worthy of it, the universe (or whatever you believe in) is going to give it to you, and you merely need to do the work to get it—then it's yours.

The concept of visualization is deeply powerful and can help you create an incredible life for yourself. It helps you focus your energy, speech, thoughts, and actions around doing everything you can to make your goals come to fruition. I personally have a great deal of experience visualizing in all three ways, and each of them truly works. Visualization works because you're more focused on what you want and are repeatedly telling your brain to believe you already have it. Overall, you're changing your expectation, then changing your behaviors accordingly to match the expectation.

My favorite tool that's fun and super easy is the vision board. You might have heard people talking about vision boards before. A vision board is a homemade collage that helps you visualize and focus on the things you want to manifest. It can be an actual collage on poster board made with glue sticks and magazine clippings, or it can be a digital collection of things on your computer you look at every day. My vision board is an elegant mixture of photos from my past that represent feelings I want more of, stock photos of places I want to go, photos of animals that embody traits I admire and aspire to, power words written in fun fonts, and heavily Photoshopped images that place me in the scenario I dream of so I have zero difficulty seeing myself in it. My vision board is one hundred percent comprised of images I printed on my photo printer at home, cut out, glued to poster board, and framed.

However you want to build yours, just build it. They work. This most recent one has me incredibly fired up. On my last one, I had images of ocean views, living in Maui, big dollars, family intimacy, retirement, health, and peace. One hundred percent of it has come to fruition.

Want to know my secrets to make it work so well? I have two. The first: I hang it next to my toilet. I'm serious. It's eye-level next to my toilet. Seeing my vision board one time a day isn't enough. I drink so much water that I'm in the bathroom *at least* five times a day. Guess what I stare at *the whole time*? I let my eyes roll over the words, drink in the grandeur of the places I plan to go and soak up the glory of the big dreams I hold. Eventually, like every other vision board, I'll stop *mindfully* staring at it and start *absentmindedly* staring at it.

This is my second secret. When the vision board starts to become part of the furniture and you don't actively see it anymore, that's when I believe it works the best. When it's just another part of the landscape, your brain expects to see it and *everything on it is normal.* This means when you're looking at your dream life in front of your face every day, your brain eventually expects to see the vision of it and expects to start living it. Your dreams stop being dreams and they start becoming a normalized *expectation* of what is and what will be. The magical part is the expectation in your brain leads to subtle changes in your behavior that ultimately lead you to do the work that *will* manifest everything on the board.

Vision boards are fun to make and can take an afternoon or a few weeks of thoughtful preparation. It's hard to do them wrong, but I would suggest not clogging up your board with quotes or phrases. These require active interaction for you to benefit, and my second secret (it becoming part of the furniture) stops working if you need to read it to gain value. Use single words to capture the essence of an idea if you intend to use words at all. These would be your core values or *ideal* core values that you're trying to adopt.

If you want to create a vision board, you can start by doing a quick Google search for "vision boards" and looking at the images section to get some ideas. You can also fire up the old imagination and start putting yourself in the scenarios you dream of.

My second favorite visualization tool? Living your desired experience, even for a day. Rent the Maserati for an afternoon. Go to the open houses of the homes you want to buy way outside your *current* price range. Vacation to the destination you want to live in (I did that, now I live here!). Go to the docks and stare at all the pretty yachts. Whatever you dream of, start getting more of it in your life, even in tiny doses. It will make a massive difference.

If you seriously want to knock this visualization stuff out of the park, actively use all three styles of visualization (mental, visual, and experiential). I challenge you to build a vision board and hang it right next to your toilet where you spend the most time looking. I further challenge you to experience something you dream of. Finally, I challenge you to close your eyes and bring what you dream of into your meditation. Fully take in what being in that moment feels like.

Volunteering & Random Acts of Kindness

You do know that giving to others is giving to *yourself*, right? I regularly give money to different groups and causes, but it doesn't quite have the same effect as actually giving my time. When you give your time, you get the privilege of participating in the solution and seeing the impact you have on others firsthand. It's irreplaceable goodness and it's hard to come across this level of awesomeness any other way.

With your local animal shelter, in addition to (or in place of) writing a check, you could:

> » Sign up to clean the kitty litter every week for a few hours.

>> Take a few dogs for a run with you every week.

>> Work the table at a fundraiser event.

>> Call for donations.

With your local planet-loving nonprofit, in addition to (or in place of) writing a check, you could:

>> Sign up to help clean trash off the beach for a few hours.

>> Take a few volunteers with you and show them the ropes.

>> Teach a class.

>> Help create an event.

Whatever your unique gifts and talents are, you can find a way to use them to help someone else and get all the warm-and-fuzzies that go with it. Recently, I posted in a Facebook group that I'd like to volunteer to coach three people in their business for an hour each. I got a bunch of responses, and I was able to help some fantastic people. Ever since, I've been getting periodic emails from the people I helped, thanking me for the work I did and sharing the successes I helped them create. It never stops feeling amazing.

THE BOTTOM LINE

At the end of the day, it comes down to input. If you're inputting bad, that's what you're going to get and it's how you're going to feel. If you're inputting good, *that's* what you're going to get, and that's how you're going to feel.

This chapter is loaded with ideas and specifics. The workbook I built for you will help you take powerful, clear action on everything in this chapter. Download it from thesixhabits.com/resources.

Your goal is to build a strong support system of good. This goodness will help you to create a life that continually feeds you the right kind of energy. To get started in the simplest way, ask yourself:

> » What can you add to your life to make it better?

> » What can you subtract from your life to make it better?

Take inventory, make new friends, get rid of the news, take a vacation from social media, and choose to focus on the good. Add in one to five good things, and you'll see a dramatic shift in your thinking and action. I promise you— the world isn't so bad after all. If you take the advice of Mr. Rogers and look for the helpers in the world, you will see the good. You just have to look.

6. Intention

Intention is the habit governing action, self-motivation, clarity, process, persistence, and prioritization. It is the habit of taking regularly planned, inspired action steps, and moving something forward, no matter how small of an increment the action is.

Intention is clear desire backed by deliberate action. Intention is getting out of your own way. The idea of intention is to move powerfully forward in the direction you choose, instead of the direction life or others choose for you. Too often, we are guilty of going with the flow and letting the tides of life push us toward a life we didn't sign up for. Sometimes we don't mind, sometimes we do. What keeps us in a life we didn't intentionally create is the fact that it's too easy to be complacent and stay put. Change is often scary, uncertain, painful, and requires effort we don't always have the time, inclination, courage, or energy for.

I have some pretty big goals in life, and without continual action, they're never going to materialize. Without a plan, I won't publish this book, I won't get to Antarctica, and I won't build my new business the way I dream of. No plan equals no results.

It's *great* to have goals in life, but without a plan and continual focus on the goals *in* the plan, you're never going to reach them. Successful plans are comprised of two major components: the big picture with its large milestones, and the tiny steps it takes to inch the plan forward. To get where you want to go in life, you need to first *identify* the big goal, whatever steps are needed to make it happen, and then create daily marching orders.

My overall plan looks like the Cheesecake Factory menu (if you haven't been there, it's more of a novel than a menu). My everyday plan looks like the daily specials at the mom & pop diner up the road. If I were to allow my daily plan to resemble the big picture plan, I'd get overwhelmed, and after a while, the list would just become part of the furniture. I wouldn't see it anymore, or in medical terms, it would become a scotoma *[sco·to·ma (skə'tōmə)—a partial loss of vision or a blind spot in an otherwise normal visual field]*. To prevent a scotoma, we need to break our goals down into the little steps. When we get overwhelmed, we lose motivation, and we tend to quit.

>> The little goals are *WHAT* you're doing.

>> The big goals are *WHY* you're working on the little goals.

IDENTIFYING AND MANIFESTING THE BIG GOALS IN LIFE

You might already know what your big plans and dreams are without skipping a beat. If you're like me, you might need to do some serious soul searching to figure out what you want out of life. I'll admit this took five years of mostly doubting myself, which was ineffective and disheartening. Ever been there? I finally broke the five-year curse by spending some time alone with my thoughts and journaling until my hand cramped up. As I mentioned previously, I took a trip to Mexico and sat on the beach alone, notebook in hand, and got real with myself. I don't know that going to Mexico was the key (as amazing as it was). I think it had more to do with keeping my phone in airplane mode and being in an environment where I couldn't avoid myself anymore. I've since expanded my solo adventures to include quiet days anywhere. I leave my phone in the car and take my notebook along for the ride instead.

When I was alone with my thoughts on the beach, I asked myself dozens of questions and finally arrived at the answer: the bakery. Prior to that, I'd done some work with a coach, I'd gone to some classes designed to help me figure out what I wanted, and none of it worked. I left frustrated and as unclear as when I started. Those things are all fantastic, and they often *do* work, but in my case, I was so crippled by self-doubt and mental fog, I needed some aggressive contemplation. I needed a long list of soul-searching and challenging *questions* that forced me to dig deep and quit lying to myself. These questions gave me freedom and clarity. They are what made the difference. Here are some you can ask yourself right now:

>> What do I most want in my life, regardless of logic?

>> What do I absolutely need to accomplish

before I die, no matter what?

» Why do I want that?

» What could I spend my time doing that would light my heart up?

» What would I do for free if I didn't have to worry about money anymore?

» What's the true thing holding me back? How can I get past that?

Start with these and create your own as you go. There are more waiting for you in the workbook online at thesixhabits. com/resources. Dig deep and investigate yourself.

More often than not, we feel like our goals aren't worth pursuing because we're destined to fail (this is the "Why bother?" mentality). The feeling of failure being destiny is typically due to the lack of a clear path forward. When defining the clear path forward, the plan must include what we will do *when* we encounter a roadblock, or we risk losing our courage to pursue what we want. That said, we need to identify the *WHAT*, which becomes the *WHY*, and from there it becomes all about the *HOW*.

When answering the HOW, you might get stuck like I do, but to get unstuck, you need to be creative and start asking yourself a lot of questions. Begin Googling. Explore YouTube tutorials. Ask people. Find a mentor. Talk it out with a friend. Chat with someone who has already done it. Look for books on the topic. Anything. Become curious and challenge yourself to find multiple ways to "solve the problem," thereby creating a wealth of options for you to evaluate. Ask the questions and the answers (along with *more* questions) will appear.

If you're a high achiever like me, this might resonate even more. High expectations carve our path forward—but also slice us to shreds. I'm guilty of achieving as a result of hating myself, not as a result of loving myself. I flogged myself into accomplishment because I would be too ashamed of any other possible outcome. Yuck. How deeply uninspiring.

As the classic Type A overachiever, I worked too hard, I worked too much, and when I dared to do such a crazy thing as take a day off, I felt bad about it. I spent so many years living in unkindness and self-flagellation that the very thought of self-care of any kind felt *wrong*.

The hard parts of *my* journey have been:

» **Lack of presence** (wanting the result *now* and feeling like a failure when it didn't materialize *now*).

» **Acceptance** (accepting my limitations and the hard days, along with the pace).

These hard parts spiraled down to:

» Lack of **kindness** to myself (saying horrible things to myself, chastising myself continually)

» Lack of **goodness** in my life (soothing my wounded soul with social media, avoidance of positive things, failure to go to the gym).

Naturally, as a result of being profoundly unhappy, I:

>> Lost sight of my blessings and **gratitude** (which made me feel even worse inside—like I was the victim when I wasn't).

Which in turn, all resulted in me losing my courage and determination to do what I wanted, and I:

>> Lost my **intention**, stopped trying, and nearly gave up on my dreams.

And repeat. The worst part? I ALLOWED IT TO HAPPEN. That breakdown is the full expression of the dark side of The Six Habits. As you might have figured out, each of The Six Habits are connected to each other. This book came exploding out of me as a result of getting *so* angry about such complete and widespread unhappiness across my life and deciding I had enough of standing in my own way. No more. Through the power of intention and the Six Habits, especially intention, we will no longer allow the bad to take over and let the good slip through our fingers.

When it comes to big goals, we need to figure them out, stand unyielding in our determination, and institute daily habits to bring them to life. Maybe your goals are simple, pure, and all about you becoming happier. Wonderful! Perhaps your goals are aesthetic and have to do with your appearance and health, so you feel better physically. Awesome. It could be that your goals are about an unfulfilled dream that can no longer sit on the shelf collecting dust. Or money, or travel, or family, or anything. Whatever it is—it's your goal, it's your life, and it's your truth! *Intention is the vehicle that's going to get you to where you want to go.*

THE LITTLE WINS CREATE THE BIG WINS

When intention is your vehicle, the fuel is all the little victories along the way. Every victory puts more fuel in the tank. Keeping track of your wins helps you see them, keeps you conscious of what you're working on, and, most importantly, keeps you attached to your why. When you train your brain to get in the habit of winning, it begins to expect it, and you perform better as your new default.

In coaching and mentoring others, I have introduced people to new work habits, fantastic productivity tricks, "life hacks," and more. Of all the tricks, tips, and strategies I've coached on, there is one that stands out as the clear winner, one that has worked for everyone. It's simple, certain to improve productivity and positive-habit building, and all but guarantees positive momentum. It is the incredible "Top 5" List.

Think of a time you were riding high on life, crushing your goals, and things were going your way. You were drunk with power, right? It felt amazing. This power is available to you when you are consistently succeeding at your tasks and stacking up the wins.

I remember when I first passed along the power of the "Top 5" list to one of my team members. It was met with skepticism and the routine smile. But then my faithful team member gave it a shot. Not only did he experience a massive transformation in his ability to be productive, but his attitude about his own productivity changed as well. He experienced a revolution in his attitude and productivity. Likewise, every other team member I have given it to over the years has experienced the same thing. It has a zero percent failure rate *when you use it.*

The "Top 5" List is something you create every single day. It is a list containing a hard limit of no more than five important items you need to accomplish *that* day. These are the most important things that must be done. These top five things support your life, your goals, your job, and consider your needs as a human. The incredible simplicity and narrow focus of the "Top 5" List is why it is so effective. It's not some big scientific formula. It's literally a top five list of things you need to do that day, assembled within a specific formula that takes your big goals into account, as well as the rest of your life.

I challenge you to create your "Top 5" List following these instructive suggestions:

> » With your big goal in mind, ask yourself: "What two small actions can I take today that will take me two steps closer to my goal?"
>   - Write your answers down as items #1, and #2.

> » With your big goal in mind, ask yourself: "What is the most pressing thing I need to accomplish today so other things will be easier to accomplish tomorrow?"
>   - Write two answers down as item #3, and #4.

» With your life in mind, ask yourself: "What critical thing do I need to accomplish today to help me be my best, happiest self?"
  • Write that down as item #5.

Questions you might be asking right about now:

» Can you vary your list?
  • Absolutely.

» Can you make your list all about the first question, the second question, or just the third?
  • Definitely.

» Can you take a day off and put nothing on there?
  • No—and this is very important. Be sure to fill your list with five things to be mindful of throughout the day. You may decide that on a Sunday with your family, your list contains things like: "Be present with my children," "Tidy the kitchen," "Go to the pool," "Ten-minute walk," and "One act of treating myself." You're active every day, and your list should reflect that, no matter how your day is oriented.

This is your list, your day, your dream, and your life. Download the "Top 5" template from thesixhabits.com/resources and get started on building your most productive day ever. Build it around you and what matters most to your dreams. On days when you need to focus less on your doing, and more on your being, let your list reflect that.

KEEPING SCORE

Finally, I want to talk about keeping track of your victories. A big part of the challenges I'm asking you to do, and the workbooks I'm inviting you to download, are all about helping you *apply* your learning. As you learn, you will have some awesome wins, and I want you to document them in a journal. This is taking your attention *away* from the mistakes and *redirecting yourself to* victories and progress. When you continually succeed at the things you set your mind to doing, be they business goals, personal development goals, or simply calling your mother more often, a win is a win. It doesn't matter how small. *Take the win.* Through the power of intention, celebrating, and recording your victories, you are saying something profound to your head and your heart: *I can do this. I deserve to win. I am a winner. I am successful.*

Your actions affirm what you want to create. *Success begets success.* When you change your relationship with yourself through your habits, you change your relationship with all that is possible in your world. These are the core principles at work here.

Success can be defined as financial success, career success, romantic success, and beyond. Success is also defined as learning to finally be kind to yourself, accepting yourself, living in gratitude, being present, getting rid of toxic energy, adding loads of goodness, bringing the power of intention to your life, and above all—being a better, happier you. Regardless of how you define success, know this: *success is not an accident only reserved for the lucky.* Success is available to all of us, and it is something you can and *will* start to create right now by accepting my challenges in this book. Yes, do the work. Yes, go online and grab all my bonus content. Yes, show up for yourself. Yes, you deserve it.

Your actions affirm the future you want to manifest. Your life is a powerful reflection of what actions you take.

At the end of the day, intention is a mindset. It is a way of thinking and a way of manifesting. If you believe you are going to win, you will. If you believe that you can do it, you can.

I want you to go hard. When you show up and bring one hundred percent to every strategy, every challenge, and every aspect of the online workbooks, you will see incredible change in your life like you've never seen before. *Real results are found in the application of wisdom, not the wisdom itself.*

I challenge you to proactively work on your habits for ninety days, including journaling every day. When you have ninety days of evidence asserting you *are* a successful person who can accomplish *anything* you decide to do—you will be blown away by the force of nature you truly are. You'll finally be able to see proof for yourself.

THE BOTTOM LINE

To powerfully decide what you want out of life is the first step toward making your dreams come true. Big goals must be broken down into little goals, and the little goals will get you where you want to go. Intention is action and is the key to the success of every assertion in this book. Intention is the heart of change.

OPTIONAL NEXT STEPS

THERAPY

I've worked with therapists over the years and they can make a powerful difference. I started working with a family therapist when I was a teenager (not my idea), and I learned amazing tools for conflict resolution, problem-solving, and sorting out my feelings. As a teenager, I was just learning the world and thinking I was independent. I thought I knew everything. I had some pretty big feelings about all of it, and I was an unproductive human across all my relationships. Basically, I was a normal teenager.

On my own (my idea), I continued therapy as a young woman. It was "proactive mental health maintenance," through my first marriage, through the start of my first company, and into my thirties. I had the same therapist through that time. What I gained from the experience was profound perspective and insight into my own feelings and thoughts. I received great insight into how to exist in my own skin as a young person. Ultimately, I outgrew that therapist and had to move on (which is a great sign of progress!), but the years I had with her were invaluable.

If I can offer you any insight on therapists, it would be this: take the time to find a good one. Find the one that suits your personality, your needs, and your level of comfort with honesty. Meet with a few so you can make an educated decision about the options available to you. It's worth it. It'll take about ten sessions to get fully invested in each other. Plan for that. Make the commitment to go at least once a month to the same person, even if your insurance changes.

Therapy and coaching are fantastic complements to one

another, as the former focuses on thoughts and feelings, and the latter focuses on action and goals. If you're not sure of the difference between a therapist and a coach, think of it like this: a therapist will help you fix a broken leg, while a coach will help you run a four-minute mile.

COACHING

I highly recommend working with a coach to hold you accountable. Find someone who fits your style, your general thinking, and whose strengths match the areas you'd like to work on. I've encountered sales coaches, business coaches, executive coaches, spiritual coaches, life coaches, and many others. I have personally worked with sales, business, and executive coaches on the professional side, in addition to life coaches for my personal life. They were not all great because I didn't know what I was looking for. My best advice is to identify exactly what you need, then seek out that specific coaching style. You'll know "your" coach when you meet him or her online or in person. Get the very best you can afford. You don't want cheap—you want results.

What is a coach? For those who haven't worked with one, it's not the sports-type coach that sits on the sidelines and yells "YOU CAN DO IT!" (though they can). Instead, they hold you accountable, help you sort out a challenge or an approach to an obstacle, help you define your action plan, embolden you to take action on your action plan, teach you things, and give you the tools to develop in the areas you wish on your own.

What is a coach NOT? Coaches are not therapists,

though they can listen to your thoughts. Unlike a therapist that will take a clinical approach, listen, and encourage you to find your own way, coaches are action-oriented and will often "cut to the chase" to help you make the most of your time together.

Do your research and be sure to check qualifications. It's not enough to like someone. Some coaches have formal training, some have experience, and some have both. Decide what's important to you and find someone who is specialized in the work you want to do and has the qualifications, approach, and style you deem important.

THE SIX HABITS 90 DAY HABIT MASTERY

The 90 Day Habit Mastery program takes the teachings of the book and the epiphanies brought to life in the workbooks then packs it all into a potent ninety-day journey of applied learning. As this book talks about repeatedly, when you change your relationship with yourself, you change your relationship with your whole world. The program is designed to facilitate that. Over ninety days, you experience twelve and a half powerful weeks of proven, habit-building activities with weekly exercises that help you cement everything you've learned into a permanent part of your automatic behavior.

Science has shown that habits are formed in sixty-six days. The 90 Day Habit Mastery program is built around this science and allows for a margin of error. It allows you to be human and make mistakes along the way, and still come out on top with new, life-changing habits. No perfection required.

The program introduces you to the powerful person you always knew you could be and the life you always wanted but never thought *you* could live. Through the program, you'll begin to finally see what's truly possible for yourself because you'll start to live it from the very first day. Over the ninety days, you will change your relationship with yourself one day at a time, and ultimately change your relationship with your whole world, every dream you've ever had, and what's truly possible for yourself.

The 90 Day Habit Mastery program is an organic graduate step of The Six Habits book and is equally fantastic as a stand-alone for those who have never read it.

Look for The Six Habits 90 Day Habit Mastery program online at www.thesixhabits.com.

FINAL THOUGHTS

THANK YOU

━━━━━━━━ ∞ ━━━━━━━━

My Dear Friend,

I'm pretty sure you believe me now when I say happiness is a choice. I want you to powerfully choose it because you finally know you can. Change your relationship with yourself by replacing your bad habits with the good ones, and your whole world *will* change.

Thank you for joining me on this journey and investing in yourself. Now it's time to take powerful action with what you've learned and do the work. Remember, *wisdom is worthless without application*. It won't be easy, but it will be one hundred percent worth it.

You're about to kick your old habits so hard that you won't even remember what it's like to be anything less than joyful. You've got this. Lean in, and don't give up.

If you enjoyed The Six Habits (or even if you didn't), please visit the website you purchased it from and write a brief review. Your feedback is valuable and will help others decide if they should read this book too.

Please write to me any time. My email address is laura@lauradibenedetto.com and I always want to hear from you if you have a question, need support, or have feedback for me. I'm committed to your incredible success and transformation, and I would sincerely love to cheer you on.

Love and Aloha,

Made in United States
Troutdale, OR
10/08/2023

13508923R10141